On Tuesday My Nipples Were On Fire: *How Autism, Hormones, and Random Strangers Stole My Sanity*

By Tami Lynn Tate

For my children: without whom there would be nothing in my world worth writing about. And for Kiernan, without whom I would not know that the previous sentence was an alliteration.

Disclaimer: This book is a true story, not a work of fiction. All characters appearing in this book are actual people and are portrayed accurately, despite their protests. Any resemblance to real persons, living or dead, is purely intentional. Also, my ex-husband's name is omitted because I am tired of that bastard suing me.

Disclaimer: All medical/ veterinary advice contained herein is solely for entertainment purposes. It should in no way be taken as professional medical advice, since the bulk of my medical training was gained by watching medical shows on cable television.

Table of Contents:

Introduction

So. I just picked up my son from his first ever trip away from home. He was at camp for a week with his school's entire 5th grade population. This is, verbatim, the conversation we had when he got into the car:

Me: "I missed you so much! How was camp?"

Carter: "Good, but something bad happened."

Me: "Oh NO, what was it?"

Carter: "On Tuesday my nipples were on fire."

I've given birth to five kids. I am neither Catholic nor Mormon, I am not crazy, and I do know "what causes that". When the kids were little, perfect strangers would stop me in public places to quiz me about my religious choices, my birth control knowledge (or lack thereof), and how many dads the kids have (they each have 1, duh...). Having a large family can make you feel like a circus freak.

My husband Kenny and I have daughters who are 20, 18, and 15, and whom public education experts have deemed "gifted"- which means they score really well on aptitude and intelligence tests, but have not a single lick of common sense between them. We have sons who are 14 and 12. Our eldest son Marshall has full-on Classic Autism and our younger son Carter has High-Functioning Autism Spectrum Disorder. These children (aka: the Tater Tots) are individually and collectively the most hysterical people I know.

After years of sharing stories about my family on Facebook and being told to write a book; I wrote a book. The only thing that keeps me sane is having a sense of humor (and also Zoloft). I am not one of those "I have autistic kids and that is now the sole focus of my whole entire life and I am going to be a giant pain in the ass about it" moms of special needs kids. I don't wear my sons' disabilities as a badge of honor and don't use them to get sympathy. Be forewarned- the majority of this book is just me making fun of my kids! Autism sucks, don't get me wrong. It is heartbreaking and exhausting and freaking horrible, but so what. Lots of things suck. We all have issues to deal with. Besides, 'normal' kids are probably really boring to have lying around the house.

I have included a handy "Tami Tate Family Tree" diagram so you can keep track of everyone. My aunt and uncle are step brother and sister after-the-fact; which is a fascinating side note but wouldn't fit into the diagram. My adult daughters are not mentioned much in this book because they are old enough to seek legal counsel, *not* because they aren't interesting or funny enough.

My Family Tree:

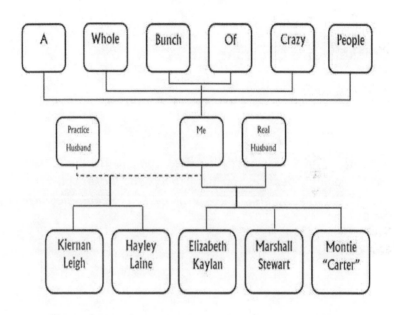

Chapter 1

Chickens are attacking me...

My 13 year old son is autistic. Like, legit autistic... Some days being the mom of an autistic child feels like being entrusted with a special soul who teaches you many things and makes you a better person. But mostly, it is just like being pecked to death slowly by a chicken.

Here is the difference between me and an autistic person: If I knock over a lamp and the light bulb breaks, I do not lick the white powder off the inside of the broken pieces.

———————

How I woke up today:

Marshall: "AAUUUGGHHHH!!!"

Me: "WHAT?"

Marshall: "What HAPPENED to you?"

Me: "WHAT?"

Marshall: "Something happened to you!"

Me: "Where?"

Marshall: "Right there."

Me: "Where?"

Marshall: "THERE!"

Me: "Where?"

Marshall: "It's terr-ble."

Me: "WHAT?"

Marshall: (now crying) "Oooooohnoo."

Me: (now awake) "POINT to it!!!"

Marshall: (points to my back)

Me: "Something is wrong with my back?"

Marshall: "This is awful."

Me (light-bulb): "Are you talking about the *tattoo* on my back? It's been there for years..."

Marshall: "This is awful."

Me: "Everyone's a critic."

———————

Dear People Who Invented the Internet:

Thanks. I know you were hoping to enable scientists and other smart people to share knowledge and research in order to cure cancer and such. My autistic kid has used it to learn the theme to 'The Flintstones' in German, Spanish, French and Dutch.

———————

Taking an autistic child with a paper fetish to Office Depot is like taking a crack head with a crack fetish to a crack store.

––––––––––

Today I am playing 'Put the Band-Aid on the Bleeding Autistic Kid'. It is kind of like 'Pin the Tail on the Donkey', only with more running and tackling and kicking and screaming.

––––––––––

Autism never takes a holiday. Usually I am happy, upbeat and able to cope just beautifully. Today, however, I am exhausted, frustrated, and pissed at the world because I do not have normal sons. Every now and then it is OK to have a pity-party and cry your eyes out at how unfair life is and how you wish you had a perfect life like all your friends have. As long as you dry it up before it's time to go pick the kids up. Letting them see mom cry is the fastest way to freak out an autistic kid. And also, the car rider ladies might think you dropped the kids off this morning and spent the whole day drinking wine and watching soap operas. Judgmental bitches, aren't they?

––––––––––

Oh. Dear. God... Marshall is watching the episode of Blue's Clues where Steve goes to college and is replaced by his "brother" Joe. He is now crying because Steve is "all gone". This episode premiered about five years ago and Marshall has seen it about a hundred times, but this single event has traumatized my autistic son more than any other thing that has happened in his entire life. I am pretty sure that if I dropped dead right in front of him he wouldn't take it this hard.

––––––––––

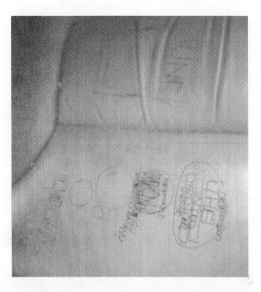

This. Is why people with autistic kids don't drive nice cars. It is the leather back seat in my Suburban.

———————

They really should invent a Rosetta Stone to teach people how to speak autistic:

Me: "How was school today?"

Marshall: "I do NOT like these boxers, I need my REAL underwear!"

Me: "You aren't wearing boxers!" (I check and he is, in fact wearing boxers)

Me: "What happened to your underwear?"

Marshal: "Somebody stoled them."

Me: "Who?"

Marshall: "I do not know who."

Me: "What did they look like?"

Marshall: "They looked like Mrs. Condren."

Me: "Mrs. Condren stole your underwear?"

Marshall: "Yes."

Me: "Why?"

Marshall: "I don't KNOW!"

———————

Just ordered Marshall's school clothes from Aeropostale. I know he would rather have his clothes from Disney, but he's a teenager now. I don't want him to be the weird autistic kid who dresses funny. I want him to be the weird autistic kid who dresses normally.

———————

Liz came home with a note regarding mandatory vaccines for her school's enrollment and she was crying because she knows that we blame Marshall's autism on shots and she was worried that she will have to get the shots and then get autism. I told her "Stop crying. We have one of those 'freaky snake handler religion that objects to medical intervention' waivers for you guys"; to which she replied "I didn't know we were that religion!" I explained that there is only one waiver, so that's the one we have to fill out.

———————

My son is screaming at me. In German. Which I do not speak, nor does he. It is going to be a long day...

———————

Unless they find a cure for autism pretty soon, his career choices will be either 'Woody Mascot at Disneyland' or 'Chippendale's Dancer Woody'.

I swear that if I ever see that "Gangnam Style" guy I am going to strangle him with my bare hands... In totally unrelated news: Autistic people love to watch catchy YouTube videos over and over and over and over and over.

Today Marshall is obsessed with opening and closing the refrigerator. Which is ironic since he is the only human on earth who will neither eat nor drink anything that comes from the inside of a refrigerator.

Marshall is yodeling. Does anyone have a muzzle I can borrow?

Note to self: Don't listen to "Red Dirt" music in the car. Having your autistic kid with an eidetic memory wailing, "Those boys from Oklahoma roll their joints all wrong- they're too damn skinny and way too long" might possibly be misconstrued as bad parenting.

———————

There really needs to be a website dealing with injuries to moms of autistic kids. I'm not having much luck Googling "I was sitting in front of him with his foot under my arm cutting his toenails and he freaked out and kicked me just perfectly so that his toes went in between my ribs and separated them and it hurts when I take a deep breath now". In other news, I have some Demerol left from my oral surgery so if I say anything ridiculous tonight it's not my fault.

———————

Stunning Moments in Autism Research: As I do most nights, I spent half of Marshall's bath time trying to get him to stop blowing bubbles with his face in the water. I spent the other half trying to convince him to let me wash his face. Then it hit me...

———————

Swimming with Marshall yesterday:

Marshall: "What is that sound?"

Me: "It's an owl."

Marshall: "What is that owl saying?"

Me: "Whooo. Whooo. Whooooo."

Marshall: (goes underwater, which apparently has the power to erase his short-term memory)

14

Me: "Whooo. Whooo. Whoooo."

Marshall: "Why are you being an owl?"

———————

You know it is bad when an entire busload of Amish people are openly staring at YOUR children in the convenience store.

———————

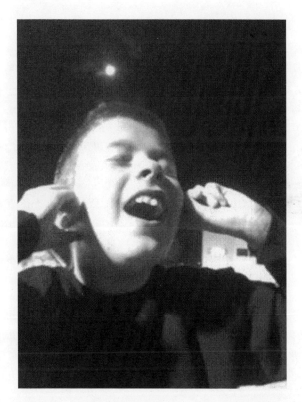

This is autism. In a packed football stadium, but also in his own small world.

This is my beautiful son - celebrating the rain.

Chapter 2

It's most definitely not OK...

I live in Oklahoma. We have every kind of weather (except hurricanes) and sometimes all within the same month! We are not all a bunch of rednecks. I would call us 'Purple' necks. We can get dressed up and behave ourselves in public if we absolutely have to; but mostly we like to sit in our yards in cutoffs, watching our kids and animals play while we drink beers. (The plural of 'beer' in my state is called 'beers' as in "I drank a lot of beers.") During the month of May each year, the sky will randomly whip itself into giant funnels and come down and try to kill us. We like to pretend that we are sophisticated students of meteorological events, but mostly we just stand on our porches watching the tornadoes and drinking beers (After we've thrown the kids and the dogs into the empty bathtub with pillows over their heads, of course). Football is a really big thing here. We pretty much all own boots, but we aren't all cowboys. It's hard to drink beer while riding a horse, so we are big on ATVs. We aren't big fans of Government Assistance Programs, but if you are truly in need we will offer you the shirts off our backs. And also beers. We love Jesus, our family, and our country. A whole lot of us are Baptists, which means we don't really talk about the beers. Here are some true stories from a state so great that Rodgers and Hammerstein wrote the best dang Broadway musical ever about us.

I saw a lady in a car at QuikTrip this morning open a Mountain Dew, reach back, and hand it to a child in a car seat. Not a booster seat, but an 'I am under 4-years-old' car seat. Nothing to see here, folks. Nothing to see...

———————

We recently had a month where we had several earthquakes in Oklahoma. We *never* have earthquakes in Oklahoma. Everyone went Bat Crap Crazy. The End.

———————

This is an ACTUAL press release from the City of Sand Springs: "The City has not moved Halloween. We felt that trying to move the date would create confusion and likely would result in two days of Halloween. Given the demands that moving Halloween would have on Public Safety and the increased risk to the public of making a change in the date, we felt that it was best not to encourage people to celebrate Halloween on a different date."

Let me translate that for you... "Halloween is on a Sunday this year and since y'all are a bunch of morons we know it's going to make everyone go monkey-ass insane."

———————

This actually happened: The lady in line in front of me at QuikTrip this morning had a $20 bill. No purse or credit cards, just the one bill. She bought a pack of cigarettes, a pop, and a Snickers. She told the clerk that the rest ($10.97) was for gas in the blue car on pump #2. Is 2.5 gallons of gas even enough to get to QuikTrip and back for smokes?

———————

The default weather forecast on my iPhone is some place called 'Cupertino'. I don't know where Cupertino is but I am planning to move there. I think I will enjoy their weather.

_____

We get married quite often around here. So it's inevitable that some of us end up married to other of us's former spouses. Which can cause a teeny bit of conflict on occasion and we aren't opposed to airing our dirty laundry in public.

_____

So the proposition to build a new fire station failed but the proposition to tear down the old one passed. Ooooo-klahoma.

_____

I just saw on the news that Sonic Drive-Ins are fixin' to start selling beer on tap. What could possibly go wrong?

_____

It is probably time to take a break from painting the porch in the July heat when you turn around to yell at the child behind you to 'get back in the house' and realize you are yelling at a Tiki Torch, whom you are fairly certain you did not give birth to.

———————

How we identify our beef and venison chili leftovers in the fridge.

———————

Just because you bought the "30 days of Unlimited Tanning" salon package does *not* mean you have to go all 30 days. This is Oklahoma, not the Jersey Shore...

———————

Here's a tip for the Sand Springs Police: If you want to catch the Meth makers spend the day undercover at Walgreens. There are always people who look like those 'Faces of Meth' posters lurking around that place. There was a lady in line in front of me today who said to the clerk "I *swear* it's been 30 days since I bought my medicine." I am not a detective, but I don't know anyone who takes 30 days' worth of Sudafed every 30 days! You would accidentally forget to take a few along the way, and therefore would not be at the damn store trying to buy more on day 27.

———————

For the first time since I got my iPhone, our forecast is better than that of Cupertino. Suck it, Apple Village.

———————

In Oklahoma, we are all friends when we drink. Put a few rednecks together, thrown in some alcohol, and you have a slap-happy bunch of BFFs. I was at the country bar with my husband Saturday, and as I coming back from the Ladies' room- a drunk guy named Roscoe asked me to marry him. I love this place. And also Roscoe. Have you met Roscoe, my new fiancée?

———————

At lunch today with my daughter. The ladies in the booth behind me are having a Margarita Lunch and taking loudly. About their husbands. One of them, I swear to God, says "...he's a lot nicer when he's drunk- so I try to keep him drunk as much as possible".

———————

I just got back from Wal-Mart. It is pretty bad when the few skinny people you see, you automatically assume are on meth.

———————

Our high school's homecoming is tonight. If you want to see what is still right with America, be there! Small town Oklahoma football: Homecoming queens dressed way too old for their age, American flags flying over the Veterans' Memorial in the end zone, little kids running around everywhere using their "outside voices, it's finally "jacket weather", and there are metal bleachers to stomp on when the band plays 'We Will Rock You'. Old women bitching about the costs of the tickets, old men coaching from the stands, and pre-teens enjoying a little freedom with mom and dad close by. We stand for the Star Spangled Banner, and pray if we *damn well* please. There are so many things wrong with our country and so many things that divide us. For a few hours on a Friday night- it's all good.

———————

I was in K-Mart for less than 10 minutes yesterday. In that time, I overheard the lady behind me in the shampoo aisle on her cell phone say, "Yeah, I'm at K-mart and then I'm going to the reading of the will. Yes, I got your pregnancy test." I get in line and the cashier was talking to the lady in front of me as she was checking her out. She was buying six items. They were *all* wildly colored bras. The customer said "I kind of have this weird thing about bras." The cashier said "Yeah, so does my husband. His favorite is my nursing bra. My daughter is nine months old and I quit breast feeding her when she was two months but I wear the nursing bra when we have sex because he says it is so *hot!*"... Note to self: Wear earplugs to K-mart from now on.

———————

Forget outlawing cell phones while driving. What we *really* need to stop is people driving with little dogs riding on their DASHBOARDS.

———————

Some people must've taken the rest of the week off. The guy in the truck next to me is drinking a beer. It is 8:30 am.

Marshall has been in 'anti-jeans' mode since Christmas break. After a knock-down drag-out, I got him into jeans tonight. I told him "YOU CANT WEAR SWEATPANTS AT OLIVE GARDEN-it's a RULE!!!" We are in the foyer waiting for a table. We have seen two adult men and one woman walk past in sweatpants. It's all I can do not to accost them and point out the aforementioned rule. Being too fat to wear jeans is NOT a valid exception.

This absolutely, as God is my witness, just happened to me at Wal-Mart. I came in through the Garden Department. In the very back corner of the outside part they had this. It is a fully grown tomato plant in a big decorative pot, with a built in cage. It has several blooms, and two bunches of green tomatoes already on it! I have Marshall occupying the entire basket, my groceries underneath, this giant plant in the baby seat, and Carter is hanging on to my back belt loop. As I am headed to the checkout, the following conversation happened:

Deceptively normal appearing woman: "Oh My Gosh! That tomato plant is beautiful, how did you get it to grow tomatoes in that little bucket?"

Me (thought bubble): OH MY effing GOD!!! Does this woman actually think this is my tomato plant from home that I have brought with me to Walmart for some reason that I can't possibly imagine?

Me: "Oh, I didn't grow it, they sell them here and I'm just now buying it".

Woke up early this morning to the charming sound of the Canadian geese that live on the little lake by my house flying overhead and honking to each other. Then I realized that it was actually just one of my cats hacking up a hair ball.

Actual Press Release: "This is the Sand Springs Fire Department with a request for citizens reporting possible fires. Due to a large amount of smoke from fires south of the Tulsa Metro area, many callers are reporting smoke and this is taxing our communications and fire run capabilities. Please report only fires in which you see actual flames or fire or smoke coming from a residence. Thank you for your assistance." In other words: "It's just a wild fire. Stop freaking the hell out! If you need to gossip about it, call your mom."

Autocorrect doesn't like the names of the cities in Oklahoma. Talala, Nowata, Chickasha, Grainola, Okemah, Heavener, Poteau, Talihina, Adair, Foyil... It makes it difficult to text people during tornado warnings- which is mainly what we do during tornado warnings- text each other trying to predict where the tornado on the ground is heading next.

Local newspaper: "Byrd ran with the pit bull still attached to his arm to the neighbor's yelling for help."

You might be from Oklahoma if for dinner tonight, you cooked: Chicken Fried Steak, Chicken Fried Deer, Chicken Fried Chicken, and Mashed Potatoes.

Dear People of Oklahoma,

   Just because it is warm enough today to wear tank tops, flip-flops and short-shorts doesn't mean you should. Getting ready for summer requires careful planning and weeks of preparation. You can't just spring those white legs, flabby arms, and gnarly toes on us all at once. I don't *care* if you have been waiting all winter to show off your new tattoos.

'Truck Testicles' are the stupidest thing in Oklahoma. And there's a lot of competition...

Lady being interviewed on the radio about the strip club in Coweta, OK being busted for back-room prostitution: "I'm glad. I don't want that stuff anywhere near me. Not near my house. Not near my kids. Not near my dogs."

I very nearly ran my car off the road when she said "dogs"...

———————

The rather large man in line behind me at the Kum & Go (yes, that is the name of the convenience store) this morning bought a 2-liter of Mountain Dew. So far, so good. Until I glance over at him after he climbed into the truck next to mine and see that he is *drinking* it.

———————

It's a pretty sad commentary on your community when you take two kids who are legally, certifiably nuts to Wal-Mart and they are the *most* normal children in the place.

———————

Went outside today. Heard a mariachi band. Upon further investigation, my neighbors are getting a new roof...

———————

Local News Story about a robbery in the Wal-Mart parking lot: "The woman told police she 'rebuked the purse-snatcher in the name of Jesus' and then began yelling for help."

May I suggest, if you should ever find yourself in a similar situation:

Step 1) yell for help

Step 2) rebuke...

———

Chapter 3

If God gave us dominion over all creatures– why are the pets in charge at my house?

We have pets. Lots and lots of pets. We have 3 dogs, 3 fish, and 4 cats. They are all mentally ill.

Has anyone besides me ever wondered what an Australian Shepherd looks like without its hair? I accidentally shaved mine bald and he is spotted and pink and about half his normal size. I'm wondering what or who to shave next! I mean, I hate to pay for a professional set of animal clippers and only use them on just the one dog…

Got this e-mail today from the pediatrician's office on Halloween safety: "All of the activity can stress out the family pet and normally friendly dogs can become cautious or fearful around the large numbers of strangers. If the dog is wearing a costume, they may be even more stressed. Instruct your children not to pet even familiar dogs."… IF THE DOG IS WEARING A COSTUME?!?!?!? What the hell?

I don't know what my husband's dog has been rolling around in in the backyard, but I hope to GOD I never step in it.

———————

The animal shelter just called. After two weeks on the waiting list- WE HAVE BABY KITTENS!!!! They will be named Tick and Tock. They were found with two litter-mates in a cardboard box that was taped shut and left on a street corner yesterday. They are about a month old. There should be a mandatory death penalty for humans who do stuff like this.

———————

Tick and Tock!

———————

Marshall: "WHAT IS WRONG WITH THE KITTENS???"

Me: (after checking on them) "It is ok, calm down... They are just sleeping."

I suppose that he thought they were dead or broken.

———————

Me: "Carter, why are you walking around the living room carrying that plastic box?"

Carter: "Because."

Me: "Because why?"

Carter: "Just because."

Me: "What's inside the box?"

Carter: (no answer)

Me: TAKES OFF RUNNING AFTER CARTER TO RESCUE THE BABY KITTENS FROM THE PLASTIC SHOE BOX WITH THE LID FIRMLY ON.

———————

Note to self: Next time a child drives you insane asking if the kitten can take a bath with him, don't underestimate the determination of said child when you finally give up and in frustration yell- "If you can get that cat into the bath tub, she can take a bath with you."

———————

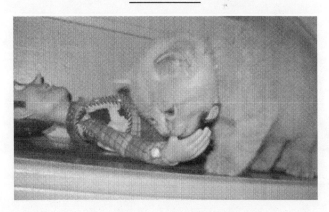

Apparently the baby kittens were boxed up and put on the street straight from their mama. Woody's thumb does not produce milk...

———————

Carter: "Does the devil live inside of Tock?"

Me: "I'm pretty sure your kitten is *not* possessed by the devil."

Carter: "What does possessed mean?"

Me: "It's when the devil lives inside of something."

Carter: "Like Tock?"

Me: "No, not like Tock."

Carter: "Then who?"

Me: "Go put your shoes on so we can leave..."

We have a new kitten! His name is Tuck (to match Tick and Tock, of course).

He was a Christmas gift for me. He hates me. The End.

Carter: "Is Tock a boy or a girl?"

Me: "A boy."

Carter: "How do you know?"

Me: "He has testicles."

Carter: "What's testicles?"

Me: "Those little balls boys have behind their pee-wee."

Carter (runs to the bathroom- comes back a minute later):

"Can I see TOCK'S testicles?"

Me: "Mhm, they are under his tail."

Carter: "Does Tick have testicles?"

Me: "Nope."

Carter: "What does *she* have?"

Me: "Nothing."

Carter: "Oh. Can I have some apple juice?"

Whew. I totally dodged *that* bullet again.

———————

Me: "Elizabeth! Don't let Tock eat that! Take it away from him!"

Liz: "Huh? He's a cat. Aren't they supposed to hunt birds?"

Me: "I am pretty sure that a breaded and fried chicken strip does not count as a bird, and he didn't hunt it; Carter left it on the chair."

———————

Sometimes things will come out of my mouth and I will think 'I swear to God- I cannot believe I just said that!' Today it was "UNWRAP THAT CAT FROM THE BUBBLEWRAP RIGHT NOW BEFORE SHE SMOTHERS!!!"

———————

We have a really cool pair of pure-bred Aussies. I thought it would be neat to take their picture in front of the roaring fireplace. This. Was the best of about a hundred photos. I give up.

———————

The next animal that sneaks up on me and licks my new tattoo is going to lose its tongue.

———————

As God is my witness, the next person who leaves dental floss where a cat can eat it is going to die a slow and painful death.

———————

Tick was spayed a few days ago. Today, without telling her what I was about to do, I told Elizabeth to fetch Tick and put her on my bed on her back. Then I whipped out teeny scissors and tweezers and took out her stitches. Tick laid there nicely and seemed glad to be rid of them. Elizabeth was so completely freaked out that she may need therapy.

———————

Kenny's using Tuck like an Ouija board to select the perfect fishing spot...

———————

Me: "DOES ANYONE KNOW WHY THIS CAT IS WET?" (Hears crickets)

Me (to Tock): "Why are you wet-and why do you smell like...vanilla?"

Tock: (no reply)

Liz: "Carter washed his hands and dried them on Tock."

Me: "Carter! Did you just dry your hands on this cat?"

Carter: "Yes."

Me: "Why?"

Carter: "Because he is like a big fluffy towel."

Me: "But if you wash your hands and dry them on the cat, your hands won't be clean anymore."

Carter: "Does Tock need a bath?"

Me (to myself): Oh. My. God. This is really my life. This. Is. My *actual life*.

———————

Just don't even *ask* me how cat pee got into my hair. I am not ready to talk about it yet.

———————

More new Kittens- Mabel and Korra.

Please don't tell anyone though- we are technically "over the limit"...

_____

Chapter 4

Naked in Wal-Mart...

Question: "Why do you make your teenage autistic son ride in the basket of the cart at the grocery store and Wal-Mart?" (I get asked this a lot. A whole lot.)

My answers:

1) "Do you work here?"

2) "Because I don't want to lose him. If he gets away from me there's a 90% chance he will not be able to identify himself; much less his missing mother."

3) "Because I can't afford to buy one of everything in this store."

4) "Because I have other stuff to do this week, and that is how long we would be here if he were walking."

5) "Because the last time I tried to let him walk, he was standing next to me in the men's shirt department and even though I was holding his hand, I was facing the other way and he managed to strip himself buck ass naked and was pointing at the Halloween shirt on the top rack that he needed and people tend to frown on naked teenagers in Wal-Mart."

*****

I am so excited that it is almost Halloween! If you have ever known an autistic person, you know why this is our *best* holiday. Marshall already has four costumes this year. They are a good investment because he will wear them all year long! He spends hours in front of the mirror admiring himself in his costumes. Carter wears his costumes and *becomes* the character. As jealous as I am of people with "normal" kids who excel at sports, academics, and all the other things that my boys are not involved in- *this* is the thing at which my sons rule!

*****

Does anyone know what in Hades 'Chayco and the Party Animals' is and where I can find it? Marshall has spent the better part of an hour screaming at me because I don't know if it is a book, a video, a computer game, a kid at school, or what. Google won't tell me either. AAAUUUUUUGGGGHHHHHHHH!!! Love the child; hate the autism.

*****

Today I am finding silver linings. My sons' autism means that they will never be drafted and die in a war.

*****

Marshall (pointing at his chin): "Something is wrong with my neck!"

Me: "It looks like something bit you."

Marshall: "Was it a vampire?"

Me: "I think it was a mosquito or an ant."

Marshall: "Did a vampire bite my neck?"

Me: "Nope, an insect bit your chin."

37

Marshall: "Why did the vampire bite me?"

Me: "Probably because he wanted to suck your blood."

*****

Autism can kiss my butt. If it were a person, I would have already beat the living crap out of it.

*****

The following words just came out of my mouth, "Marshall! You have to wear underwear; we are going to Olive Garden."

*****

Fact: People with Autism do not sleep in hotels. So neither do people without autism.

*****

There must be a lot of autistic savants who narrate baseball games. Where do they come up with these statistics? 'Such and such team has nearly won the World Series in 24th inning with 3 balls and a runner on 3rd when the temperature was 79 degrees 5 times in the past 92 years.' This sounds like Carter talking about Thomas the Train & Friends ad nauseam... (ad nauseam is Latin for "until I am nauseated".)

*****

I know that people think I am scatterbrained, irresponsible, bitchy, or weird. But in defense of myself- having autistic children is the actual reason. Within the first five minutes of walking in the door with my sons after picking them up from school, here is what

38

happened: Marshall dropped his backpack inside the door and I fell over it. Carter then fell on top of me since he was following me too closely. I picked up myself and Carter and went into the kitchen to tell Marshall to hang up his backpack. He was just putting into his mouth last night's Braum's chicken which he had fished out of the trash. While I am separating him from said chicken (which made him cry) Carter comes running in with Tick the cat who is choking. So I give the kitty the Heimlich and she pukes a green eraser onto my new fake UGG boots. As I am cleaning the puke off said boots- Carter tells me that there is Kool-aid all over the floor. As I am cleaning up the Kool-aid and putting the trash onto the front porch, Marshall falls down because he's trying to take off *his* boots. As I am helping Marshall take his boots off, Carter comes in from the bedroom with a box that came in the mail today and which contains a present from Santa. As I am putting said box in the closet- I decide I have to pee. Right. Now. As I am sitting down to pee, I step in sticky cappuccino which was apparently in the bottom of the cup in the bathroom trash which the dog knocked over last night. Now I'm going to start laundry and homework and wait for my daughter to get home from the bus stop and tell me what a hard day she's had at middle school.

*****

Thing I said to Marshall today: "I don't *care* how close to the toilet it is located- the shower curtain is not for wiping your poopy butt on." This is why we can't have nice things...

*****

No matter what you are doing this afternoon- I don't care if it's a colonoscopy, root canal, dinner with your ex-husband, dinner with *my* ex-husband, recovering from brain surgery, or sitting in the car rider line, I will trade you. All you have to do is take two autistic kids to the dentist.

*****

39

One odd thing (just the one) about autistic people is that they are excellent mimics. I would love to know what the Latina dental assistant thought when my non-Hispanic autistic son started speaking to her in an exact imitation of her thick Spanish accent.

*****

One of Liz's best friends is getting harassed at school by some thuglings. I get the general impression that she would gladly kick some butt on his behalf, if she weren't half the size of a normal seventh grader. It would probably be like getting attacked by a pissed off Chihuahua. Note to bullies: Don't mess with the sibling of a special needs child- they have a finely honed sense of justice and will take your ass *down*...

*****

There are two things that every autistic person on earth should be permanently banned from owning. Number one is a firearm.

This is number two.

*****

This is another of those *"Tami Tate! There is* no way *this is a true story"* stories. I have witnesses; it's 100% true. Carter is in 6th grade this year which is no longer elementary, but has all the 6th graders in our district in one building. I am asking him the first week if he has classes with his friends from his old school or if it's all new kids, and if he's made any new friends. He says he's already made two new friends, named Jo-Jo and Boy. I automatically assume that since he has an auditory processing disorder that he has just misunderstood their names. He tells me that Jo-Jo is actually named Joseph, so I buy that one. Then we discuss this kid he is calling "Boy". I tell him the kid's name is "Boyd with a D" and he just didn't hear the D at the end. In an effort to encourage my son to not be the weird kid, I tell him to make sure to call the kid BoyD and not Boy, because it might make the new friend unhappy to be called "boy", which is not a name.

Yesterday, I ask Carter how school was, and he says "Boy doesn't like being called Boy with a D". He tells me that "Boy" has been suspended for hitting Chris. I ask why BoyD hit Chris and Carter says "because he couldn't reach me". It seems "Boy" got frustrated with the discussion over his name and said "Call me 'Boy' one more time," and Carter did. BoyD couldn't reach Carter, who was two desks down, so he hit Chris who was within hitting range. I try, to no avail, to explain the concept of sarcasm to Carter. Another week passes and I totally forget about the friend with the dubious name. We go to 'Meet the Teacher' last night and meet the teacher of these children. I repeat all the aforementioned conversations to her and… wait for it… she informs me that the kid is ACTUALLY NAMED BOY.

*****

Marshall is in full-time Special Ed class with nine other kids. When I dropped him off this morning, there was a very loud cricket in the classroom. The End.

*****

41

Trying to put Chap Stick on an autistic kid is like trying to put Chap Stick on a cat. Only harder. And with more spitting, scratching, and hollering.

*****

Took Marshall to see the 'Wiggles Live' show today. I have never seen so many autistic boys in one place in my entire life. Obviously Marshall had no idea that "going to see The Wiggles Live" meant that he was going to be in the same room as the *actual* Wiggles from TV. The look on his face when they came onstage was priceless! We had aisle seats and the Wiggles do a bit where they walk through the audience. Jeff (the Purple Wiggle) stopped suddenly at our spot and shook Marshall's hand. I think his life is now complete. If Keith Urban (who is my "if I could totally get away with it" man) came off stage and French-kissed me, my smile would only be half as big as Marshall's. Worth. Every. Penny.

*****

I keep lists upon lists in my head of all the things I am going to do when my kids get older and things slow down. Yes, I *am* deluding myself into believing that such a time will come. I'm adding volunteering to help with Special Olympics to my list. Carter played softball this year and had a great time! Thank you to all of the people who make these trips possible. It is such a challenge for my family to go out of town with our two "special needs" kids. I cannot imagine taking a whole group of someone else's. Some of the kids have physical disabilities that add to the logistical challenge. It always amazes me that there are people in this world who seek out kids like ours to spend time with. They are such a blessing to us, but I forget that they also bless people who aren't family. My boys have never been invited to spend the night at a friend's house, but thanks to these awesome folks they've had a trip away from home without their parents!

There were also some generous local business people who donated money to supplement the funds that the teams raised all year. The kids each got dinner and a t-shirt from Eskimo Joe's (Kenny asked "Carter-where'd you get that cool shirt?" Carter said "from the Eskimos") in Stillwater, Oklahoma where the Oklahoma games were held. To all the coaches, sponsors, helpers, and donors-THANK YOU ALL!!!

If you are reading this and you find yourself in possession of a few extra dollars this year, please consider donating it to your local schools' Special Olympics team. Even if you can just give enough to buy the kids all a pop or a bag of chips, it will bless their parents so much.

*****

Chapter 5

It's a Rule: Look it up...

I am just a little neurotic so I have lots of rules. I reserve the right to make up New Rules as needed. As long as everyone follows these few simple rules, I will be happy.

Rule #1: Unless I have given birth to, or exchanged vows with you, or you have been to medical or dental school; there is simply no acceptable excuse for you to be in my personal space.

———————

New Rule: If you aren't old enough or tall enough to use the stove, you aren't allowed to bitch about what I cook on it. I had one kid just crawl up on a barstool, peer into the pan, and inform me that my fried chicken has too much pepper. Five minutes later, another child informed me that she had chicken for lunch. Oh, and she also wishes that I could make "more interesting" side dishes to go with it.

———————

New Rule: If you wake me up at 3:45 am because you peed in your bed; you do *NOT* get to complain about the color of the clean sheets I put on it.

———

New Rule: If you puke on my socks, you have to lay down for the rest of the day. I don't care if "puking fixed the problem".

———

Ok, let me be more specific: We don't *skip* in the house while carrying scissors either.

———

Don't tell a non-compliant child *"We are just going to have a Mexican Stand-Off then..."* unless you are prepared to explain what a 'Mexican Stand-Off' is.

———

New Rule: If someone you don't know sends you a text, don't automatically assume it's a person with the wrong number and be a smart ass and answer their "How are you doing? I love you" text with a detailed description of how you're doing and an "I love you too"- because there is a slight possibility that the person did not, in fact, have the wrong number, but was replying to a *group text* sent by your teenage daughter to *both* of her long-divorced parents. I will give you a minute to work that out in your head and see why Rule #7 is: NO MORE GROUP TEXTS!!!

———

New Rule: Always think things through *before* you act. Otherwise, you could find yourself naked in the shower with a very sticky nest of baby spiders stuck to your fingers, shaking your hands and shrieking to no avail. Baby spider nests look like a floofy little cotton ball but they are actually made of super glue. Don't pinch them out of the shower windowsill.

————

New Rule: When explaining to someone that the reason you cut all your hair off was because "it was getting way too long for my age- like, I am talking 'Pentecostal long'", it's always a good idea to make sure that one of the two people with whom you are making small talk is not a legit Pentecostal.

————

New Rule: If you have to get up to pee in the middle of the night and the house is completely dark and your mom is in the bathroom already, don't stand outside the bathroom door in the totally dark hallway not making a sound. Especially if you are a child. Kids are creepy enough at night as it is.

————

New Rule (applicable if your age ends in the word 'teen'): if you can't remember to take a house key with you, you will not be allowed to leave the house. Period.

————

New Rule: If you wake me up an hour before my alarm clock is set for; you do not get to practice amateur psychology and attempt to diagnose the deep-seated reasons for my bad mood.

Ms. Cole,

Please excuse Elizabeth's tardiness. Her mother is neurotic and couldn't sleep because she was worrying about Carter being in Stillwater for Special Olympics... She simply does not possess the mental capacity to simultaneously obsess about one child and get the others to school on time. AKA: she doesn't have her shit together...

—Tami Tate

New Rule: Don't ask me to write you a tardy note unless you're willing to be expelled.

New Rule: You are never too old to stand in the corner if you smack the cat. I don't care if she scratched you first. You started it by dicking with her, so *you* get to go to 'Time Out'.

———————

New Rule: No matter how nervous your son's 105 degree fever during the night makes you; don't go online to check WebMd. I don't think that guy is even a real doctor.

———————

New Rule: Don't text me from the bathtub. *Especially* if you live in my house and I am paying for the phone- and the bath water.

———————

New Rule: If I've been up all night with you because you are sick; you do not get to complain that my breath is stinky.

———————

New Rule: If you bring me teeny screw-top bottles of wine; you do not get to make fun of me for drinking out of the teeny screw-top bottles. If I wanted to get all fancy and drink from a wine glass I would've asked you to bring me a *box* of wine.

———————

New Rule: If you are too sick to go to school; you're too sick to text me screen shots of online medical journals describing serious illnesses that I can *promise*-You. Do. Not. Have.

———————

Wearing false eyelashes to a high school football game when you're over 30 just makes you look desperate.

––––––––

Act your age. The world is overpopulated with adults who live too vicariously through their teenaged kids. My advice to them- go out with your own spouse. Do all the things that being over 21 has earned you the right to do. Let the *teenagers* be teenagers. You had your chance; if you screwed it up, sorry. There are no do-overs.

––––––––

Thing I read in the news today that seemed like a bad idea: *"She was planning to go to Pakistan to meet a man she met online..."* The story did not, of course, have a happy ending.

––––––––

Do not ever. Never. No matter what. Search Google Images for 'Spider Bites'.

––––––––

New Rule: It is perfectly acceptable to chase one of your children down and steal their 'Kid's Meal' toy *if* it's a Wonder Woman tiara and you've wanted one for over 35 years. The only crying allowed is tears of happiness.

––––––––

New Rule for Politicians: If you do not have a vagina- don't ever, ever, ever, never talk about women's issues. Period.

————————

If you aren't willing to properly parent your children- then don't have them! I am amazed at the stuff that seemingly sane people let their kids and teenagers get away with. The only time they get involved is to bitch when their kids do something wrong- and even then they feel sad that little Timmy won't be their friend if he gets punished. You want to know why I am always so stressed out, exhausted, and driven to delirium by my children? It is because I am actively parenting twenty-four hours a day. Even when they are not doing anything wrong I am watching them and guiding them. If you let them listen to "gangsta rap" and watch a bunch of inappropriate crap on TV and play video games that aren't even remotely age appropriate then you forfeit the right to complain when they emulate the thugs and violence you've paid to expose them to. Seriously.

————————

New Rule: The next child who decides that finding cat puke in the hallway is enough of an emergency to wake up their mother at 4:45 am is going to die a slow and painful death in torturous agony. I don't care if the cat is on fire. Just throw him out the front door *quietly* and let me freaking sleep.

————————

New Rule: Nobody is allowed to drink out of Mommy's "special cup" this evening...

————————

New rule: If you bring your kids to my house for Halloween candy-don't put your cigarettes out on my porch. I can probably get someone to pull your DNA off your discarded butt and track you down. I won't, but I totally could.

New Rules: If you eat through the wood fence and run a mile from home dragging your girlfriends with you; you are getting stuck in the garage till your dad gets home to fix the fence. I don't *care* how much you bark. If you poop on the living room floor, you are grounded from your iPad and computer until tomorrow. I don't *care* how much you cry. I am in charge here and these are my rules.

Chapter 6

Alcohol may have been involved...

Disclaimer: I get rip-roaring drunk about once every three years. I have a lot of little people that I'm normally responsible for so even though I talk about drinking a lot, I don't really do it very often. I'm the daughter of an alcoholic so I am not stupid about it. I know exactly what the consequences are and what my limit is. Jesus is ok with it. Seriously, we are cool... Baptist Jesus even.

Things I learned this weekend:

1) Being twice the legal drinking age and twice the legal blood alcohol level involves a lot of math.

2) If you develop an aversion to wine, Jack Daniels is a really good substitute. But it's not one for one (more math) and also maybe not as classy.

3) If you talk while Sam Harris is singing, his mom will turn around and give you a dirty look.

4) Everyone is your friend in the bathroom of a bar, even when you are old. Seriously, the friends you make in the ladies room are the most loyal and also the most complimentary ones you'll ever find.

5) Eating at a pancake restaurant at 2 A.M. is just as fun when you have your own kitchen and can make yourself pancakes as it was in college when you couldn't.

6) Don't piss off your designated driver unless you can walk to the car really fast even if you can't walk to the car really straight.

7) "Drunk Kenny" is still my favorite guy of all time ever! (Kenny is my husband, who is really fun when he's had a few too many. Not that he's *not* fun sober, but you know what I'm trying to say here...)

8) I should always wear red because it is in my "color wheel" and matches my hair color, eye color, and skin tone. This, according to the "Professional Colorologist" I met in the ladies' room.

9) Mel McDaniel died in 2011.

10) The greatest gift God ever gave me is that I did not have a cell phone with a camera and Facebook when I was in college.

§ § §

The reason my 14 year old daughter can't keep her room clean (today's version): we have a "crappy dustpan". I use it almost every day with no problems but apparently her bedroom floors are some kind of specially-special hardwood that renders the dustpan inoperable.

§ § §

Carter: "Why did you just put chemicals all over my face?"

Me: "It wasn't chemicals, it was just Vaseline and I didn't put it all over your face, just under your lip where you are licking it and making a clown mouth."

Carter: "What is Vaseline?"

Me: "It's just petroleum jelly."

Carter: "What is petroleum jelly?"

Me: "It's a chemical by-product from when they make crude oil into gasoline."

Damn, foiled again.

♫ ♫ ♫

Kenny's office had a get-together last night:

Conversation #1-

Person A (Whom I have known 16 years): "Tami, have you met (Person B)?"

Me: "No. (Shaking hands) I'm Tami Tate, Kenny's wife- it's nice to meet you!"

Person B (Whom I have never laid eyes on): (Simultaneously) "Yes. We live next door to each other."

Conversation #2-

Me (To Kenny:) "I finally met (Person B) from next door who works with you."

Kenny: "You know, you might actually know people if you ever left the house."

Me: "I know lots of people on Facebook..."

Conversation #3-

Liz: "So, how was the party?"

Me: "It was good. It was kind of socially awkward though."

Liz: "*It* was socially awkward or *you* were socially awkward?"

♫ ♫ ♫

Husband: "Uh-Oh Marshall. I can tell how your day went. It's not even 7 o'clock and your mom is into the wine."

§ § §

I tend to be a Libertarian, but... I think they should pass a law that says that all boxed wine boxes must be see-through. Think about it.

§ § §

Carter (YELLING): "Mooooooommmmm- the toilet is overflowing!!!"

Me (mumbling): "Well, of course it is since Dad's at work."

(Fast-forward 5 minutes) Me: "Carter! Is this poop or puke?"

Carter (YELLING): "It's just poop."

Me (mumbling): "Wow, I called that wrong."

§ § §

Marshall is fascinated with the Old Navy mannequins and greets them like long lost friends.

§ § §

How I woke up thing morning: I was sound asleep flat on my back when a kitten jumped onto my throat and dropped a sock onto my face. You can do the math.

§ § §

Carter, upon getting out of the tub: "I am going to freeze to death."

Me: "You are not going to freeze to death. You're cold because you just got out of the bathtub."

Carter: "No, it's because you buy cheap towels."

Me: "Everyone's a critic..."

§ § §

I think I just dislocated my shoulder trying to unhook my bra. When you hit a certain age (40), you lose so much flexibility that your body can't accomplish things your mind knows that you can. I was helping Kenny unload firewood last month and when we were done, I was getting ready to jump off the bed of his truck. My body completely froze and, even though I could picture myself jumping three feet and landing safely on the ground, I suddenly had no idea how to make that happen. After much contemplation and trying to remember the things I learned in physics class in college, I ended up sitting on my butt, scooting to the end of the tailgate, and reaching one tippy-toe down to the ground and then kind of sliding the rest of my body onto my feet. I probably should bust out those yoga DVDs I bought. After I make one of the kids climb up on a stool and get them down off that high shelf in the bookcase...

§ § §

You know how, when we were kids and went to the public pool (because no one's moms worked so none of us had our own pools and now it seems like every time your kids spend the night with a friend they are packing a bathing suit), the pool manager made you take a quick shower before you could swim? Well, I just left Wal-Mart and I was thinking that if they had those there as you came in it would be a positive thing. And for those few of us who actually took a shower before we left home, we could grab a quick one on the way out because... germs.

§ § §

If I were a gay man, I would totally trademark the term "Dick Dynasty" and then get rich. Very, very rich.

§ § §

True. Story. I was irritating Kenny today and he finally had enough and said "Marshall! Go punch your mother in the nose." Marshall walks calmly across the room, smiling big enough that I assume it's a rare moment of clarity where he is aware it was a joke and is in on it, but I am totally wrong and it is just a moment of autism equals 'I take everything literally', and before I can even react, my son punches me in the face. I know I can't let him see that he has actually physically hurt me, so I cover my face until my eyes quit watering and show him that I am ok. Kenny tries to figure out how to get onto his son for hitting a girl (when it was his own fault) and comes up with nothing, so he pretty much just had to let it go at "don't hit your mother *even if* I told you to."

§ § §

If one more person asks me "where is such and such random item I haven't used in two years but simply must have right this second?", I am going to jump off my roof. Why am I the only human in my house who has to be responsible for each and every thing ever owned by each and every person and has to know at all times where all the damn things are located?

$$\text{\wedde \wedde \wedde}$$

The three ways in which I have almost died today and it's only 9:30 am:

1) I was in the Junior High hallway after walking Marshall to class when the bell rang and hordes of inattentive teenagers who are taller than me were unleashed. As I came around the corner from the Special Ed room, a rapidly moving boy almost ran into me. He was carrying a pencil at waist height and the sharp part hit me in the stomach. If I were not wearing two shirts and a hoodie- I would have been impaled. Of course, the child rolled his eyes like it was *my* fault. I have to daily resist the urge to treat other people's kids as if they were my own and thusly reprimand them.

2) I was taking a bath this morning and the cute little kitten who was perched on the edge and dipping her paws in like she wanted to take a bath too did not, in fact, want to take a bath too. I have about a half box of Band-Aids stuck to my midsection and hands now.

3) I was cutting a bagel with the first knife I found, which was the very hugest butcher knife in the block, when one of the cats stepped on a talking Buzz Lightyear in the living room and he made a siren sound and shouted at me which caused my blood pressure to rise to a dangerously high level, and also caused me to nearly sever an artery with the aforementioned knife.

$$\text{\wedde \wedde \wedde}$$

Today is the premiere of the new 'Hunger Games' movie. Liz and her friends are going to a marathon of both movies this evening. They are "loosely dressing like the movie characters" for school today. Here is a conversation from last night:

Liz: "Katie said I should bring my bow and arrow to school tomorrow."

Me: "Yeah, because a legit, non-toy bow and arrow set totally won't get you suspended for the rest of your life and me sent to jail."

Liz: "I told her it was *probably* a bad idea."

§ § §

For anyone wondering what kind of wine goes with taco-flavored Doritos... The answer is Cabernet Sauvignon. You're welcome.

§ § §

Q: "How hard is it to break into your house?"

A: "I just did it in 3 minutes after I locked my keys inside as I was leaving to pick up the kids from school."

Q: "What did your animals do?"

A: "Not a damn thing."

Q: "Were you injured?"

A: "Well of course I was."

Q: "What did Kenny say?"

A: "I haven't told him yet."

Q: "Is this even the weirdest or most exciting thing that's happened to you today?"

A: "Not even close."

Q: "What was?"

A: "When Tock moved the vacuum cleaner that was blocking the door to the closet in which the panel that contains the bathroom plumbing is located and which is open because Kenny has been working on it and the stupid cat got inside it and then got himself stuck under the bathtub."

§ § §

I hate jeans with shiny crap all over the butt but can't seem to find any without at least a few rhinestones. I just wiped my hands on my back pocket and ripped my hand open on a stupid bedazzle. Apparently I am not even safe around my own clothing.

§ § §

Sitting at the table tonight with Liz helping her with homework and being poked to death by an underwire, so I wriggle my bra off from under my shirt and hang it on the back of a chair without a second thought.

Liz: "WOW! That is a huge bra!"

Me: "Thank you."

§ § §

Take a container of Cool Whip, a block of cream cheese, a can of pumpkin pie junk, and 1/4 cup of powdered sugar and whip it all together with an electric mixer. Grab a box of graham crackers and prepare to be extraordinarily happy.

§ § §

Annoying Yoga DVD Teacher: "This thigh stretch is great to perform in the shower where the hot water can help lengthen the thigh even further."

Me: "Yeah, except I've already fallen over twice doing it here in the living room. I landed on the couch the first time, and did a *very* attractive combination flamingo hop and arm windmill trying to avoid toppling over onto the hard wood floor the second time. If I tried this in the shower, my family would find me unconscious or dead and also naked- which would not be a positive event. So shut up so I can hear the weird sitar music..."

♪ ♪ ♪

I worked really hard to clean the aquarium today. The fish all showed their appreciation by dying.

♪ ♪ ♪

I'm sure when other people hear the African language opening lines to the "Circle of Life" song from the Lion King being sung by one of their children at the top of their lungs- they think it's charming. I, on the other hand, immediately take off running toward it because I know it means a kitten is being held aloft by its armpits.

♪ ♪ ♪

New exercise plan: I have moved the box of wine to the basement refrigerator. Think about it.

♪ ♪ ♪

The "Air-Ride Suspension" has gone out on my SUV, so the back end now sits about a half foot lower than the front. The ride is *really* bouncy, so of course, Marshall bounces up and down on purpose when we stop- to keep the fun going- which makes us look a car full of Mexicans cruising around in a low rider! The good news is, I don't have to jump to get into it any more.

Dear The Political Correctness Police: Seriously- there are whole clubs of low riders that the Mexicans started. It's a hobby, not a racial stereotype.

§ § §

Ready.

Chapter 7

There's snow place like home...

In 1880-81, a rare six-month long series of blizzards held the people of DeSmet, South Dakota near-prisoners in their homes. With the heavy snow piles blocking supply trains, and the town not yet established enough to have much in the way of food stores, the people nearly starved to death that long, long winter. Through sheer force of will, and by the grace of God, these hearty pioneers managed (barely) to stay alive until the snow finally stopped.

In January 2011 a very rare series of snowstorms hit Northeast Oklahoma. The snowfall amounts were huge by Oklahoma standards, and as soon as one round of snow would melt, another would hit. Oklahomans are hearty people, but were ill-equipped for the unexpected hardship of having public schools closed for days at a time when their kids were supposed to be back in school after being home three weeks already for Christmas Break. There were even several days where the snow was so deep that the men were trapped in the house with their wives. As a result all the people went bat-shit crazy. The following is my diary from that terrible season:

Sunday, January 9, 2011 at 1:47pm CST

How do you know you are pathetic? When the way you know it is snowing at your house is to read it on someone else's Facebook. I missed the part where it was supposed to snow today! It is pretty to look at though.

Monday, January 10, 2011 at 8:37am CST

Dear My Neighbor Down The Hill: I know my truck doesn't really belong in front of your house, but that is where it slid to. I will come get it when the weather improves. Try not to hit it when you slide into your driveway tonight.

Wednesday, January 12, 2011 at 10:02am CST

Trying to put gloves on my autistic kids this morning is the most challenging thing I have ever done. Ever. I think I could get tiny little gloves on feral cats easier. And the cats wouldn't cry on the way to school because they can't eat Lucky Charms with gloves on.

Thursday, January 13, 2011 at 9:19pm CST

I'm teaching my daughter to two-step in our socks on our living room wood floors. She isn't old enough to drink beer, so it is really not going so well...

Wednesday, January 19, 2011 at 5:07pm CST

Picked up the kids and then stopped by the grocery store to get just a few things. Apparently '2-4 Inches of snow' is some kind of code for 'holy shit, something apocalyptic is fixin' to happen and we are all gonna starve to death and run out of toilet paper and pop'! Wal-Mart was just way too crowded and chaotic for my nerves to handle today.

Monday, January 31, 2011 at 8:10am CST

Apparently everything that can fall from the sky (except locusts and frogs) is going to do so tomorrow. I have heard the weather guys call for: rain, freezing rain, thunder-snow, thunder-ice, sleet, snow and blizzards. So basically we all need to duck. Or get drunk.

Monday, January 31, 2011 at 3:47pm CST

Picked up the kids and during the hour I spent in and out of the car, the weather forecast went from 'Winter Storm Warning with up to 12" of snow' to 'Blizzard Warning with up to 18" of snow'. What is the next stage of panic after blizzard? Since when does Oklahoma even *have* blizzards?

Monday, January 31, 2011 at 4:38pm CST

They aren't even parsing words at this point. The weather forecast is now officially calling for a 'Shitload of Snow'.

Monday, January 31, 2011 at 5:10pm CST

Meteorologist Travis Meyer just said the phrase "twenty inches of snow". With a straight face...

Monday, January 31, 2011 at 10:19pm CST

I'm thinking this snow thing is a hoax. I don't see any snow. It's kind of a let-down after the whole "twenty inches" forecast thing.

Monday, January 31, 2011 at 11:03pm CST

Holy Crap! It is *thundering* and sleeting torrential ice!!! I have never seen such a thing. This is pretty cool!

Tuesday, February 1, 2011 at 7:12am CST

Today the snow is "Australian Shepherd belly" deep. Which means my dogs cannot figure out how to poop in the yard. I would feel sorry for them if it wasn't so freaking funny!

Tuesday, February 1, 2011 at 12:49pm CST

It is a really good thing we have Facebook so that we can see other people's pictures of snow. Since there is only one foot of it at my house...

Tuesday, February 1, 2011 at 3:30pm CST

The weatherman just said that he "doesn't see any way this snow will be able to melt at all in the next 7 days".

Tuesday, February 1, 2011 at 10:21pm CST

Wheat thins, canned cheese, and Boone's Farm Strawberry Wine almost make being snowed in doable.

Wednesday, February 2, 2011 at 9:05am CST

Today, I am thankful for electricity.

Wednesday, February 2, 2011 at 10:25am CST

Yesterday, snowed in. Today, snowed in. It is almost like Groundhog's day...

Wednesday, February 2, 2011 at 1:55pm CST

Is there some kind of contest to see who can make it out of their house first? Where are these nimrods all trying to go? There are men in trucks sliding down my hill and they do *not* look like they are going anywhere important.

Wednesday, February 2, 2011 at 6:40pm CST

Autism silver lining #74: Marshall is not even remotely aware that we are snowed in. He has not been forced to get dressed and go to school. His computer and TV work. He is happy.

Thursday, February 3, 2011 at 1:40pm CST

Here is the difference between men and women: I am in my pajamas cooking homemade stew inside where it is warm. My husband is in 25 layers of clothes in 10 degree weather shoveling the driveway (even the parts that the car doesn't drive on).

Thursday, February 3, 2011 at 2:23pm CST

I eat when I am stressed, tired, or bored. They are probably going to have to cut a hole in the side of my house to get me out when this is over.

Thursday, February 3, 2011 at 7:26pm CST

I wonder why they can't invent some kind of snow plowy thing that drives around melting the snow with a big hair dryer. I know it would make a lot of ice and water, but surely there is an engineer who can figure out all the piddly little details and make this happen.

Thursday, February 3, 2011 at 7:56pm CST

I hates the Wiggles. All of them.

Thursday, February 3, 2011 at 8:59pm CST

Today I watched my neighbor dig his car out of his giant driveway, pull it out into the street, get it stuck, dig it back out, get it unstuck, pull it back into the driveway, and go inside. I think it might be a few more days before we get out. This is hopeless. How long was it before the Donner Party started eating each other?

Thursday, February 3, 2011 at 11:32pm CST

Elizabeth just asked me how long I thought we could live on the food we have at home before we are all dead if we stay snowed in. I told her a week. She looked in the pantry and said that she thought we could go much longer. I told her that we would all be dead because I would lose my mind and kill us myself way before we ran out of food. It took her a minute to realize I was joking.

Friday, February 4, 2011 at 9:57am CST

I just saw the weather forecast: 2" of snow today, 2" of snow on Sunday and 4" of snow on Wednesday. Are you *kidding* me?

Friday, February 4, 2011 at 9:59am CST

Dear Mother Nature,

   I have exactly 11 Zolofts left. Just thought you should know that.

Love, Tami

Friday, February 4, 2011 at 10:07am CST

You know how an animal caught in a trap will chew its own leg off to get free? My husband is currently shoveling the *street*.

Friday, February 4, 2011 at 2:22pm CST

The mail truck is here. To stay apparently. It's stuck.

Friday, February 4, 2011 at 4:32pm CST

Free to a Good Home: Children. (For photos and descriptions please email tamitate@stopsnowingrightthefucknow.net)

Friday, February 4, 2011 at 8:37pm CST

So. It snowed four inches today and nobody even noticed. Any other time this would have been the lead story on every channel. We have lost all hope.

Friday, February 4, 2011 at 8:42pm CST

My husband is reading the weather forecast online and making a crazy little laughing sound. I am worried that he is losing it.

Saturday, February 5, 2011 at 12:22pm CST

I would love to hear someone say "My name is ____ and I'll be your waitress this evening"...

Saturday, February 5, 2011 at 12:48pm CST

I shaved my legs, tweezed my eyebrows and put on a bra and makeup for the first time in a week. If anyone needs me, I will be in my front yard throwing myself at the first man who drives by in a four wheel drive vehicle.

Saturday, February 5, 2011 at 2:06pm CST

I just put gloves on my autistic son so he could go play in the snow. It took longer than the C-section by which he was born and I was cussing, sweating, and bleeding afterwards in both instances.

Saturday, February 5, 2011 at 2:11pm CST

Why, yes. Marshall's gloves *are* rubber-banded on with Ziplocs. Only because I have no zip-ties. Actually, the only reason his hands aren't stuck together at the wrists right now is because I have no zip-ties.

Saturday, February 5, 2011 at 6:01pm CST

I left the house with my husband and kids for dinner and to get DVDs from the Red Box. Then I was driven right back home. Home sucks.

Saturday, February 5, 2011 at 9:12pm CST

It's pretty sad when you consider renting movies at the Redbox machine "going somewhere".

Sunday, February 6, 2011 at 2:27pm CST

Dear Mother Nature,

I just spent 2 hours (and half a mortgage payment) with my kids at Wal-Mart. We got enough groceries and magazines to last another week. While we were shopping, Daddy got a truck-load full of firewood. Bring it on bitch; you don't scare me.

Sunday, February 6, 2011 at 4:42pm CST

Sand Springs schools have just announced they will be closed again Monday. My sense of humor about this situation is gone. I am sorry, but did I sign anything saying I wanted to home school my kids? I don't think so.

Sunday, February 6, 2011 at 4:47pm CST

If anyone needs me for anything, I will be busy killing myself.

Monday, February 7, 2011 at 1:49pm CST

I do not really need another request to join anything related or pertaining to 'Autism Awareness'. I am pretty much as aware of autism as I am ever going to get.

Monday, February 7, 2011 at 5:22pm CST

Just saw the weather forecast. Even more snow is headed our way. This is what I get for calling Mother Nature a bitch.

Monday, February 7, 2011 at 5:29pm CST

Maybe before the snow hits, we can all swap kids with each other. At least then we can be snowed in with different children which will be a little better than being snowed in with the same ones from last week.

Monday, February 7, 2011 at 11:18pm CST

I am beginning to think that I like the *idea* of winter more than I like *actual* winter.

Tuesday, February 8, 2011 at 6:43pm CST

School will be closed again tomorrow. Dear School: How 'bout you just let us know when you are ready to start again? Then we won't have to check every day. Stop getting my hopes up.

Wednesday, February 9, 2011 at 12:19pm CST

What are your top three things to do when this crap is over? Mine are: 1) Refill Zoloft. 2) Roast myself in a tanning bed. 3) Date night with my husband in a place where you have to be at least 21 to enter.

Wednesday, February 9, 2011 at 2:44pm CST

My parents live in the middle of absolute nowhere. They had 20" of snow last week and another 20" today. I think my sister and I will soon be coming into some life insurance money since they are snowed in together and that house ain't big enough for the both of them.

Wednesday, February 9, 2011 at 3:54pm CST

Sigh. More snow. How can there even be this much water left on the Earth?

Thursday, February 10, 2011 at 11:02am CST

-14 degrees this morning, and 67 forecast for next Thursday. Oklahoma.

Thursday, February 10, 2011 at 11:35am CST

Stop running in the house. STOP running in the house. Stop RUNNING in the house. Stop running IN the house. Stop running in THE HOUSE. Stop, oh to hell with it. When are they going back to school?

Thursday, February 10, 2011 at 2:01pm CST

"Oklahoma has recorded all-time record low temperatures this week." Even though it has stopped snowing, they have cancelled school until Monday because of the dangerously low temperature. This is just adding insult to injury.

Friday, February 11, 2011 at 8:10am CST

From the *Tulsa World*: "Tish, an artist from Owasso, said her children have been productive during snow days. Her 9-year-old twins and her 6-year-old son have made Valentine's Day mailboxes, knitted baby caps for children in third-world countries, and played in the snow." In other news, Tami Tate's kids have sat in front of the TV in their pajamas eating junk food all month. If I ever meet this 'Tish', whom I assume is also skinny, I'm gonna bitch-slap her!

Friday, February 11, 2011 at 1:26pm CST

I think that illegal immigration won't be a problem if we have very many more winters like this one. Who would leave sunny Mexico to come to this godforsaken place?

Friday, February 11, 2011 at 4:19pm CST

IT'S MELTING! IT'S MELTING! IT'S MELTING!!!!!

Sunday, February 13, 2011 at 6:23pm CST

You know you have a problem when your mom calls you to make sure you are ok because she hasn't seen you on Facebook all day. And you are 40 years old.

Chapter 8

I am too drunk to get married...

At my first wedding, I was too young to drink. At my second wedding, I was too pregnant. Therefore, I can't blame it on the alcohol...

Poll question: Am I the only human still alive who, as a child, was given a frozen raw hotdog wrapped in a paper towel as a delicious summertime snack?

———————

I think that thin ankles are a marvelous blessing. No matter how much weight you gain, you still have one really great feature.

———————

OK. I would *totally* give it up for a bag of Fritos. Is that considered prostitution?

———————

My son just climbed onto my lap and started petting my eyebrows. I know I have let the personal grooming slide lately, but *seriously*?

———————

For all you fetuses out there: Patrick Swayze was *our* Edward, Jennifer Grey was *our* Bella, and Dirty Dancing was *our* Twilight. There were no giant wolves, but the music was really great!

———————

Political Correctness gone awry: I just heard a reporter refer to two of the candidates for new Pope as possibly becoming the first "African-American" Pope or the first "Latino-American" Pope. Neither of these men are, nor have ever been, Americans.

———————

This Kenny and I at our wedding. I am 4 months pregnant. We're in the kitchen of the bed and breakfast after the reception with our drunk wedding party eating the leftover food. I know people pay lots of money for perfect, professional wedding photos, but I prefer real-life shots. This is my favorite.

———————

Life lesson learned: I am having a crap-tacular day. The dentist says I need five fillings and a crown, none of which I can afford within the next decade. The driver side window and door handle are broken on my car so I have to exit the passenger side all day. I stop at Quiktrip for tea on the way to retrieve my children from school and find out the old man who was in front of me in line has paid for my drink. For $1.07, you can make another person's whole day all better.

———————

I have never played real-life golf, but I've played enough Wii Golf that I could make a living as a commentator on the Masters' Tour.

———————

I just hate it when someone yummy catches your eye, and after some quick math, it dawns on you that you're old enough to be his mom and it goes from "he's kind of cute" to "I'm kind of creepy".

———————

I used to love to wear new clothes while they still *smelled* new until I learned that the smell is from the formaldehyde they put on the fabric to keep it from mildewing on the trip overseas from the country in which it was assembled. There *is* such a thing as too much knowledge.

———————

I dreamt last night that my entire back was tattooed in Disney characters. I really, really need for these kids to hurry up and get grown before I *totally* lose my sanity.

———————

I took a road trip into the state of Arkansas and discovered that they have way better road-kill than Oklahoma. It was like going to the zoo! Only everything was dead.

———————

If you really want to prove to yourself how inadequate you are, spend a few days and plant a garden. Then try keeping it alive long enough to grow actual vegetables. Then imagine that the survival of your family depends on your ability to grow their food. My family is so dead.

———————

I am watching the *'History of the Mafia in Cuba'* with my husband. I have realized that the extent of my previous knowledge of Cuba comes from watching *'Dirty Dancing 2: Havana Nights'*.

———————

Facebook got stuck when I was updating my profile picture on the "drag thumbnail" part. It now has a close up of my boobs as my entire photo. I am not seventeen. This isn't what I was aiming for.

———————

I've had an epiphany. My first act as President, assuming I win, is to work a deal with Nutri-System where *they* provide all the food for adults on food stamps. If they can send delicious, healthy, perfectly-proportioned food to ladies on diets, they can send it to fat people who don't work.

———————

I have this new thing I do and I am wondering if I am just a freak or if y'all do it too? When I am putting on my makeup or brushing my teeth and looking in the bathroom mirror, I use my hands to lift my chin, pull up my eyelids, pull back the skin on my cheeks to show my cheek bones, and pooch out my lips to see what I would look like with a facelift. I didn't do it even once until I turned 42. Now I do it at least twice a week. FYI, with a facelift I would not look like a younger version of myself. I would look like an entirely different person. It's a good thing I cannot afford plastic surgery.

––––––––––

You know you are the parent of an actress when John McCain is on TV and your daughter asks "Isn't that the guy who auditioned for President?"

––––––––––

Step 1) Go to McDonald's

Step 2) Buy a pumpkin pie

Step 3) Bring it home, turn it upside down, and fill the ensuing divot with whipped cream

Step 4) Live Happily Ever After.

––––––––––

I totally want to get a bumper sticker made with "HOW AM I DRIVING?" and the phone number to call will be my ex-husband's.

––––––––––

Me: "I might be a little less bitchy if I didn't spend the first hour of my day with people whining, complaining, and yelling at me."

Kenny: "Maybe you shouldn't listen to Talk Radio when you get up."

I was speaking about his *children*, but he does have a point!

———————

I don't really understand why people are so opposed to gay marriage. What they ought to be opposed to is celebrity marriage.

Chapter 9

Shut up and drive...

Because I am neurotic- I drive my children to and from school each day. "Car Rider" lines are Karma's way of getting back at me for every bad thought and deed I have ever had or ever will have. I spend two full hours each day getting people to and from school, half of which includes my spawn being in the car with me. The following are my musings while waiting in the Car Rider Line and transcripts of actual car conversations with my children:

The argument I just lost:

Carter: "What is that thing?"

Me: "It's an air freshener."

Carter: "It smells like poison."

Me: "It doesn't smell like poison. It smells like Apple Spice."

Carter: "It's poison."

Me: "It's not poison. It's air freshener."

Carter: "Can you eat it?"

Me: "NO! You cannot eat it!"

Carter: "If you eat it will you be dead?"

Me: "Probably."

Carter: "Like poison?"

Me: "Yes, like poison..."

Carter: "I told you it smelled like poison in here."

*****

I have finally been driven crazy by my children. I spent the entire car ride home engaged in a heated debate with an autistic child over whether or not Plankton from Spongebob is a pickle. (He is, in fact, not a pickle). Although I was right, after I reduced my son to tears, I was forced to concede that Plankton is a pickle.

*****

Liz: "What is Good Friday?"

Me: "The day Jesus died."

Marshall: "Why did Jesus die?"

Me: "He died to make up for our sins and so that we can go to Heaven after we die."

Marshall: "Who is Henry the Octopus?"

Me: "The purple puppet on the Wiggles."

Liz: "Well, that was random..."

Driving my kids to school is like being on a game show, only without the cash and exciting prizes.

*****

Carter: "Why do airplanes have wheels?"

Me: "For the same reason birds have feet?"

Carter: "Birds have feet?"

I now have a bruise from hitting myself on the forehead.

*****

Liz: "I'm going to shoot my bow after school today."

Me: "Awesome! Maybe you can get good enough to go deer hunting with it!"

Liz: "Why would I shoot a deer?"

Me: "Um, so we can eat it."

Liz: "I don't like deer meat, maybe I can shoot a cow?"

Me: "No, that's illegal. There aren't a lot of roaming wild cows."

Liz: "Well there should be because they taste way better!"

Me: "What about duck hunting?"

Liz: "Ew. I know... CHICKENS!"

Me: "You can't shoot people's chickens either. Just shoot at the barn for now and we'll get you a hay bale to practice on."

*****

In the car this morning: (Marshall's verbal stim is really bad lately)

Marshall: "Where are you taking me?"

Me: "To school."

Marshall: "Where are you taking me?"

Me: "To school."

Marshall: "Where are you taking me?"

83

Me: "To school." (repeat for 10 minutes)

Marshall: "Where are you taking me?"

Me: "To Crazy Town, since that's where *you* are taking *me*..."

Elizabeth: "Is there an actual place called 'Crazy Town' or is that from a song?"

*****

Driving Elizabeth to her first orthodontist appointment. We are chit-chatting (which basically means she is running her mouth while I pretend to be interested) and she says, I kid you not, "Well, it won't be too bad since he won't be looking at my teeth."

*****

Tate driveway this morning:

Me: "Marshall! Get in the car!"

Marshall: "What?"

Me: "I said Marshall get IN the car!!!"

Marshall: "It's Steve."

Me: "Ok, *Steve* get in the car."

Marshall/Steve: "What?"

Me: "I said 'Steve, get IN THE CAR!'"

Marshall/Steve: "No."

Carter: "Mom, make Steve get in the car."

(That saying about how God gives special needs children to special moms is crap. He gives special kids to moms who are already crazy themselves.)

*****

We just heard an update about a missing baby in Missouri on the news. Liz said: "If you're going to kidnap someone, it's pretty smart to kidnap a baby because they can't call the police or anything."

*****

I see a lot of bumper and window stickers on cars since I spend half my day in the car rider line. I would like to publicly inform my entire family that after I am dead they had better not even *think* about having tacky white "In Loving Memory Of" window decals made for their cars. Everyone has dead relatives. Every. One. It's *not* a fantabulous way to honor the memory of your dead mother/father/spouse/child... it's just creepy.

*****

Marshall: "What are you doing?"

Me: "Rubbing my eye- it's itchy."

Marshall: "Did you get pink eye in a ball pit?"

Me: "What?"

Marshall: "What?"

Me: "Carter, do you know what he just said?"

Carter: "He's imitating SpongeBob."

Me (Still thinking 'WTF?'): "Well, now it makes perfect sense."

*****

Driving on the highway- trying not to die in a fiery crash. Marshall lets out a blood-curdling-slam-on-the-brakes-because-someone-is-in-mortal-danger scream from the back seat:

85

Me: "WHAT IS WRONG???"

Marshall: "My eyelashes are missing!!! Did you cut off my eyelashes?"

*****

Family Thanksgiving Road Trip: With absolutely no warning or commentary, Marshall spit one of his molars out. Onto his sister... This photo was taken 10 minutes after everyone was done freaking the hell out!

*****

Instead of jail, convicted felons should be required to drive for a week with an autistic kid in the car. There would be no more crime. Ever.

*****

Marshall:
"AreyoutakingmetoschoolAreyoutakingmetoschoolAreyoutaking metoschoolAreyoutakingme toschool?"

Carter (Screaming): "YES! WE ARE GOING TO SCHOOL! STOP ASKING HER!"

Liz: "Man, someone woke up on the wrong side of the bridge this morning."

*****

Does anyone *else* keep tweezers in their car so they can work on their eyebrows in the car rider line because the light is so much better than home?

*****

Today I had one of those precious moments as a mom when you realize that the lessons you have tried to instill in your children are actually sinking in. Marshall was singing the Spongebob song in German and Carter yelled at him "Marshall, this is AMERICA, we speak ENGLISH!!"... sigh... I am choking up. All these years of Conservative Talk Radio in the car on the way to school are finally paying off.

*****

I watched a teenager texting and driving this morning. Driving a MOTORCYCLE. And texting. Just wow.

*****

Liz: "So that's Cloud 9? Wow, it doesn't look like much."

Me: "Mhm... WAIT! What did you just say?"

Liz: Repeats above comment.

87

Me: "HOW do you know about Cloud 9?"

Liz: "From some kids at school. That's where they have the pole dancers and drunk guys watch them dance around naked, right?"

Me: "Pretty much."

Liz: "Well, I expected it to be a little fancier looking!"

*****

I am going to start selling ad space on the back of my Suburban. I spend so much time in it sitting still that I should at least give the people behind me something to read.

*****

Marshall: "HACK...COUGH...hack..cough...HACK...cough...cough..."

Carter: "MOM! STOP THE CAR!! You need to put Marshall in the trunk!"

Liz: "You know what's weird about oranges?"

*****

Listening to Lady Gaga's 'Judas' on the way to school. Liz asks "What is she saying?" So I start talking about Judas, who betrayed Jesus with a kiss before he was crucified. And then I tell her the Easter story. She listens intently to this diatribe, I'm expecting some profound questions. Instead, she says "MOM! I meant, what are the *lyrics*? I just couldn't hear the words because Marshall is talking too loud!" Mom = Fail.

*****

Listening to a Prince cd:

Liz: "*What* are you singing?"

Me: "'Little Red Corvette'."

Liz: "I thought it was 'liiiii-iive it correct'."

Me: "Why would it say that?"

Liz: "Because the song is about trying to be a better person."

Me: "The song is about a girl that's a big old slut and he wants her to settle down and be his girlfriend."

Liz: "Then what does the car have to do with anything?"

Me: "It's a metaphor about the girl; she's fast and dangerous like the red Corvette."

Liz: "I hate metaphors- it's like being in English class instead of listening to music."

Me: "Well would you rather the song just be called 'You are a Dirty Whore'?"

Liz: "Yeah, that would be a lot more straight-forward."

Me & Liz: (singing to the tune of Little Red Corvette)... "You're a diirrrr-errrrr-teee whore...."

*****

Liz: "You know how that song 'Ring around the Rosie' is about the apocalypse- so is..."

Me: "Wait. That's stupid. It's not about the apocalypse!"

Liz: "Yes it is, everyone knows that- but my question is- is 'London Bridge is Falling Down' about a terrorist attack?"

*****

I had every intention of making today a "Normal People" day. The car ride to school shot that all to hell:

Marshall: "Cough...hack...Cough...Cough..."

Carter: (singing Lady Gaga's 'Born This Way' at the top of his lungs)

Liz: "I had the most realistic dream last night. I dreamt I had some horrible disease that makes you go blind. I was pretty upset because if I'm blind then I won't be able to see what clothes I'm wearing and if they match or not. And I will have to read those books with the little dots with my fingers."

*****

Not sure when it happened but when a car honked at me I used to assume it was someone checking me out. Now I automatically assume that something is awry with my car.

*****

Liz: "How many girls do you think I'll see today at school with shorts and UGG boots on?"

Me: "You guys should play the slug-bug game but instead of Volkswagens, hit each other when you see the shorts and UGGs."

Liz: "We call them Eski-hos..."

Me: almost wrecked the car and killed my whole family I was laughing so hard.

*****

How to freak out a car full of kids in two easy steps:

1) Announce that your nose is bleeding.

2) Let one of them see the bloody Kleenex.

*****

Me: "Look over there at all those goats!"

Liz: "Are they wild?"

Kenny: "Yeah, there are roaming packs of feral goats all over Oklahoma..."

*****

Me: "Carter! Quit biting your nails!"

Me: "Son, seriously. Get your hands outta your mouth!"

Carter: "I have to bite them so that you won't cut them with clippers."

Me: "Then you should bite your toenails because I hate cutting those for you!"

Liz: "Ew... people don't bite their toenails!"

Me: "My ex-husband used to sit on the couch and do it all the time."

Carter: "What's an ex-husband?"

Me: "Let's all stop talking in the car, please."

*****

Saw a little turtle in the road this morning on the way to school. The following conversation ensued:

Liz: "Can we keep him?"

Me: "Yeah, when I come back by if I can find him and if I can catch him we can put him in the back yard."

Liz: "I'm pretty sure if you can find him then you can catch him...."

*****

Marshall (to Carter): "Why are you all red?"

Carter: (Assumes he's bleeding to death, instantly freaks the hell out, and nearly strangles himself on the seatbelt trying to get to a mirror)

I turn around and sees this:

Chapter 10

I can't cut your neck off if you don't hold still...

Kitchen conversation:

Me: "Would you please hold still?"

Me: "I said HOLD STILL!"

Me: "I can't cut your neck off if you don't hold still!"

Elizabeth: "MOM!"

Me: "What?"

Elizabeth: "Are you talking to a dead chicken?"

Me: "Um, I guess so?"

Eliz: "You are so weird..."

I have a Facebook friend who posted a well-thought status about the events in the Middle East today. She received no responses. I have another Facebook friend who posted a status about how her period cramps are particularly bad this month. She has over 40 responses so far.

———

The definition of irony? A toothless old man at the gas station just told me I have a beautiful smile.

I thought working out was supposed to make people all endorphiny and happy? It just makes me bitchy, hateful, and out of breath.

I just bought a new bra. While wearing pajamas. Sitting in a recliner. The Internet is freaking AWESOME!!!

This morning I had unplanned oral surgery. In the last 11 hours I have ingested (per dentist's orders): 6 steroid tablets, 6 antibiotic capsules, 8 ibuprofen, 4 Tylenol, and 2 Demerol. All on a stomach with no solid food in it. My husband seems to think this has affected my personality somewhat, but I am not sure WHO IN THE HELL ASKED HIM FOR HIS F*^KING OPINON!!!

Spent 12 hours in bed and slept 6. In the good old days, that would've been quite an accomplishment. Nowadays, it's because I have too many kids and my cats are nocturnal.

Kenny was at the University of Oklahoma football game in Norman tonight when the stadium lost power. We were talking about it when he came home:

Me: "If I was at that football game, I would be terrified that the power outage was a terrorist attack!"

Kenny: "You're always terrified that *everything* is a terrorist attack."

Me: "Not always. Sometimes I'm terrified that weird stuff happens because Jesus is coming back."

———————

Conversation with a genius:

Liz: "Why are you laying down?"

Me: "My ear is on a heating pad. I have an ear infection."

Liz: "How do you know?"

Me: "Because it feels like someone is stabbing me in the ear."

Liz: "Why don't you look in it with your otoscope like you do with us?"

———————

I woke up with a strange man in my bed. It's Marshall. He's absolutely the strangest person I know.

———————

Some people have calendars that tell them when they need their hair recolored. I have kids:

Carter: "What are you doing?"

Me: "I'm fixing my hair."

Carter: "Why?"

Me: "So it will look pretty."

Carter: "Oh, I thought it was because it's turning all black."

Took myself to the movies tonight to see "Some Other Movie That Isn't the New Twilight Movie Because Even Though the New Twilight Movie Is My Favorite Besides Dirty Dancing I Have Already Seen It Twice Since It Came Out Ten Days Ago". Alas, there was no such movie. Maybe next week I will see "Something That I Haven't Seen Three Times"...

When mom has OCD: Today I walked down the hallway, noticed it was filthy with waist-high smudges from little hands, started cleaning it, realized there was no end to the filthiness, decided to touch up the paint, realized I last painted three years ago and I am out of that color paint. I load up kids and go to the paint store, buy paint in two shades darker than the original color to hide the dirt, tape and paint the hallway, step back to admire my work and see I've painted my entire hallway the color of dirt, and realize I'm a genius. I forgot completely what I went down the hallway for six hours and $65 ago.

I spent four hours on the business end of a shovel today. You know it's been a good day gardening when, at the end of it, your bra is full of dirt.

So, Madonna shows her naked boob on stage. On purpose. She is 53. When I was a kid someone always had a senile old lady in their family who couldn't remember to keep her clothes on. Usually that got the relatives whispering about "putting her in a home".

———————

Dear Lord, help me not to get mad at stupid people today, but to remember that I am possessed of superior intellect and that thinly veiled condescension is perfectly acceptable.

———————

In addition to jury duty, I have *always* wanted to be a "Nielsen Family" and do the TV journal so my choices count towards their ratings. I have finally been selected and my week starts today. I don't keep the TV on for company during the day- I run a live stream of talk radio on my iPhone instead, and my primary TV viewing consists of two things: American Idol and DVRed re-runs of Gilligan's Island and the Love Boat. They are going to be soooo disappointed when they get my results.

———————

First "date night" with hubby in over five months tonight. Someone could get hurt.

———————

Queen: 'Somebody to Love'. One of those songs that you hear in the car and do such a kick-ass drum solo on the steering wheel that you start to worry that the airbag might go off in your face.

———————

Today I played a rousing game of "Why Does the Upstairs Bathroom Smell So Bad?" Two hours on my knees and one trip to the store for more bleach later, I am going to have to break it to my husband that he's going to have to take the toilet out so I can clean properly behind and under it; we need to tear out and replace a section of the sheetrock in the wall that is a few inches to the side of the toilet; I'm going to repaint the bathroom and replace the vinyl tiles in that corner and then we are going to put a lock on the door and no one under four feet tall will ever be allowed in that place again. Geez Louise. It's a penis, not a high-pressure fire hose.

What a glorious day. The sky is blue. The sun is shining. The birds are singing. Now if only those stupid birds would shut up so I can go back to sleep and enjoy it.

Do you ever have days where you don't fix your hair or wear makeup, then do laundry and clean house until you look like a meth head, only with teeth, and not skinny? And you hope that you won't pass away today because even the undertaker won't be able to make you look presentable? Or is it just me.

So you know how when you first fall in love with someone and they're all shiny and new and your heart gets all fluttery just thinking about them and you can't wait to see them again and you tell all your friends how perfect they are and how you've finally found 'The One'? But then the 'new' starts to wear off and you start to notice little things about them that aren't perfect, and the fluttery feeling goes away, and you start to notice all of their faults for the first time, and you don't want to tell anyone because then you'll look stupid for being so overly enthusiastic at first. This is the story of me and my love affair with the new Reasor's grocery store. I've been there 6 or 11 times since it opened, and it's been the highlight of my year. I was there yesterday and Reasor's and I had our first fight. It was really crowded, which made how small the store is painfully obvious for the first time. They decided not to enforce the dress code I suggested, so there were people roaming around in old t-shirts and flip flops. The bakery was out of the little cupcake shaped cookies that I use to bribe my daughter into doing stuff. I had to wait to check out for the first time, and the people in front of me were being ugly to their kids *in public*. The produce department's big sale this week was plums, which are gross. The little tomatoes that come in a bunch were all mushy. No nice employees were loitering in the main aisle asking me if I was "finding everything okay". The cashier wasn't smiling and didn't act thrilled when I asked for paper bags. I had to wait to get out the door because so many people were dicking around coming in and getting carts, which made me think that the entry way is too small. And ALL OF THE BAGGED SALADS WERE FROZEN! This is my all-time biggest grocery store pet peeve so I had to buy lettuce the old fashioned way - and it wasn't on sale. I hope this doesn't lead to a messy divorce. I'm running out of options now that I split up with Warehouse Market, Wal-Mart turned into a meth head hooker who needs a bath, and Homeland is suffering with bi-polar disorder...

Interesting fact I learned today: as I was reheating a bowl of last night's edamame in the microwave, I saw that they were shooting out sparks... According to Google, this is because they have a high iron content and it causes arcing just like if you put any metal into the microwave. They suggest you reheat them on the stove like you boil them. This just confirms what I already knew- eating vegetables is stupid.

Today, my husband used "Tami Tate" as a verb.

———————

Liz: "How much weight have you lost so far?"

Me: "10 pounds, why?"

Liz: "Because I can kind of tell..."

Me: (launched myself across the room and held her in a smothering bear hug and kissed big wet sloppy kisses all over her cheeks and forehead.)

Liz: "Ew! Now I have to wash my glasses, you got lipstick all over them."

Me: "It wasn't lipstick it was spit! You're my favorite child."

———————

One of us just got off the treadmill. The other ate an entire box of Scooby Doo fruit snacks...

———————

I'd nearly forgotten how hot Yul Brynner was in 'The Ten Commandments'.

———————

Nacho Cheese Doritos are one of those things that, when you haven't had it in a long time are quite good. Them. THEM. I meant "when you haven't had *them* in a long time."

———————

If the rest of my day goes anything like my morning so far- I'm going to end up either in 'Protective Custody' or 'Under Medical Supervision'.

———————

I am starting to take it personally that I am over 40 years old and I have never been called for jury duty. I watch enough Dateline that I would make a *perfect* juror.

———————

The neighbor kid just brought home the dog that *isn't* the one that is missing. It's been that kind of day.

———————

Kenny is out of town for a three-day fishing excursion. Liz and I are doing something scandalous! We each have a window open and the AIR CONDITIONER is running!!!

———————

Q: "Why are you eating Frosted Flakes for lunch?"

A: "Because I'm the mom, so I can. Plus, it was either that or Tequila shots."

———————

What a coincidence! I was totally just thinking that I wish I could mop the bathroom floor at 12:38 am.

———————

I exercised several times a week and tried to eat better all summer. I lost a total of two pounds. I have had food poisoning since Monday. I've lost five pounds. This is just Karma laughing her ass off at me.

———————

Since Elizabeth is allergic to peanut butter, I decided to try making no-bake cookies with Nutella. You know how they have to cut open the side of morbidly obese people's houses and forklift them out...

Nutella No-Bake Cookies:

2 Cups Sugar

2 T. Cocoa Powder

1 stick Salted Real Butter

½ Cup Milk

1 Cup Nutella

1 tsp. Real Vanilla Extract

3 Cups Quick Oats

Directions: In a saucepan, bring to a boil the butter, milk, cocoa, and sugar. Let boil for 1 minute without stirring. Then turn the heat off and quickly add the Nutella and vanilla and stir until melted. Add the oatmeal and stir quickly but thoroughly. Drop the mixture onto the waxed paper by heaping spoonfuls. Wait until the cookies are cooled and hardened. Eat them all really fast before your family sees that you've made them.

Chapter 11

Illness, injury, mayhem and madness...

I don't have kids. I have evil little harbingers of pestilence, misery, and despair.

I am always amazed at how precariously the micro-society that is the Tate household is balanced on the edge of chaos and anarchy. Mom is under the weather one morning and within an *hour* the inmates have taken over the asylum.

‡ ‡ ‡

Ok, I can understand needing a Band-Aid because you've got teeny hands and you've stapled your index finger, but ten minutes later needing another Band-Aid because you have stapled your *other* index finger?

‡ ‡ ‡

When you wake up puking (and there is not a fetus involved), you know it is going to be a sucky day.

‡ ‡ ‡

I distinctly remember when my kids were babies and had ear infections (five kids, all with bad ears= approximately 1,000 sleepless nights) saying "I wish they were big so they could just tell me what is wrong instead of crying all night long". I was wrong. I'm currently being kept awake by Liz, who has an ear infection. I woke myself up every two hours last night to check her fever because she had a headache and I am terrified of meningitis. This morning I took her to the doctor and then bought insanely overpriced antibiotics. I finally got to sleep at midnight, and she woke me up 30 minutes later because her ear hurts and she can't sleep. After I had her take Advil and eardrops and put a warm rag on it, and advised her to stop whining so loudly because if she wakes up her brothers it will not be pretty. She pronounced "*You* aren't the one who has to deal with this!" Dear Karma: Seriously?

‡ ‡ ‡

I hate it when people whine on Facebook about their medical conditions. Except when I am sick. Then it doesn't bother me so much.

‡ ‡ ‡

My lymph nodes and spleen are enlarged. Webmd says I have a virus and not to worry. Take that, nObamacare! I have a totally free doctor...

‡ ‡ ‡

I'm not sure how I even got myself into such a situation, but I just explained the Caesarean section procedure to my mildly autistic son, at the conclusion of which he burst into tears assuming my stomach *remained* cut open. So I had to show him my scar. Which completely grossed out my daughter, providing me with a 'safe-sex' speech opportunity during which I explained to her that if she got pregnant, the baby was coming out one of two ways. And both require stitches.

‡ ‡ ‡

Whomever said "drugs and alcohol don't mix" never chased a Lortab with a glass of boxed wine.

‡ ‡ ‡

Autistic people have a tendency to *way* over exaggerate any minor health concern. Marshall has a dry, hacky cough. It's like a chain-smoking coal miner with pneumonia has moved into my home.

‡ ‡ ‡

Thing I am most grateful for today: I let Carter eat Nerds candy instead of dinner. It was way more pleasant when he later threw up in my hand.

‡ ‡ ‡

There is a commercial for that medical alert button necklace that old people wear when they are home alone which ominously warns that "One in Three Older People Will Fall and Injure Themselves This Year." I believe it! I fell over this morning and bruised my leg when I hit the wooden hamper. I was doing something extremely dangerous. I was putting on socks.

‡ ‡ ‡

I am 42 years old. I have a cold and feel like dog crap. I want my mom to come feel sorry for me and bring me some mashed potatoes.

‡ ‡ ‡

I have finally identified *the* most dangerous object in my entire house. It's a tool used for making lemon zest. I've had it for a few years but this evening is the first time I've used it. It has the added bonus of, after it removes the top layer of skin from your hand, it immediately douses the wound with lemon juice.

‡ ‡ ‡

Pediatrician: "So, what makes you think Marshall has strep throat?"

Me: "When his throat hurts he chews on things. Yesterday at school he ate both cuffs and the pocket off his shirt."

‡ ‡ ‡

Weird things that happen during flu season- one of your kids wakes up with a fever and you start praying he has strep throat.

‡ ‡ ‡

So. In Sand Springs, we have a lot of sand in our yards (go figure). The grass grows a ton of really pokey 'Goat's Heads' in order to reproduce itself. They come into the house on the feet of my family and wind up in the carpet and occasionally the laundry. This morning, there was one hiding inside my washcloth. I seriously wish I had found it at the *beginning* of my shower and not at the end (when you wash the last place you wash when you take a shower). If anyone needs me, I will be standing up with my legs crossed today.

‡ ‡ ‡

I'm going to start a homemade mashed potatoes, chicken and noodles, and Sprite delivery service for sick people. I am going to be *so* rich.

‡ ‡ ‡

My mom has been texting me twice a day since we got sick to check on us. Today I told her I think I have tuberculosis and need to go stay in a sanitorium. Autocorrect kept changing it to *sanitarium*. Which is way more accurate at this point...

‡ ‡ ‡

I've read that the Tulsa and Oklahoma City coroner's offices are backlogged, so I'll save my family the wait for an autopsy report and just give my mysterious cause of death in advance. I was cleaning the bathroom with bleach, had an asthma attack (the kind where you go in 2.4 seconds from humming the theme song from *Beauty and the Beast* to "Oh my god I feel like I've been holding my breath underwater for days and my lungs are exploding"), ran to my bedroom nightstand for my inhaler (where of course it was not located) but which alerted all the cats that something exciting was happening and they needed to haul ass to run straight at me as I'm running to Liz's bedroom for her inhaler, so we all collided in the hallway. Now I'm lying on the couch dying from either the asthma or the heart attack. And then the cats will eat my hair.

‡ ‡ ‡

Taking a photo of the hole in the roof of your mouth with an iPhone is actually not as easy as it sounds.

‡ ‡ ‡

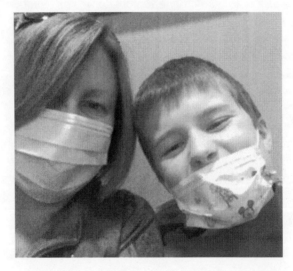

Good news! The Doctor says it's not the flu!

Chapter 12

To Whom it May or May Not Concern:

When I have something to complain about to a business, celebrity, or anyone else who would benefit from some constructive criticism, I mentally write them a short letter. I don't actually send them, but it makes me feel like I am doing my part.

Dear ABC Television Executives,

I've just finished watching *Soft Core Porn with the Marginally Recognizable*. Oops, I mean *Dancing with the Stars*. Your show is no longer "family-friendly." Hell, it isn't even "normal-adults-who-wear-clothing-on-a-regular-basis-friendly".

《·》

Dear Fellow Sand Springs Citizens,

P.O.D.S. are designed to be filled with your extemporaneous crap, picked up by a giant flatbed truck, and carted away to a climate-controlled warehouse. They have commercials that clearly demonstrate this entire process. P.O.D.S. are *not* meant to be a cheap alternative to building a spare room onto your house. Seriously, when you have to weed-eat around it and your dog has given birth to puppies under it- that's a little too white-trashy, even for Oklahoma.

«·»

Dear Person with the Bed for Sale on Craigslist,

You might want to re-word your advertisement. Saying "the bed really hasn't had very much use" could possibly be misunderstood.

«·»

Dear People Who Print Signs for a Living,

My pet peeve is when people use apostrophe "S" incorrectly. Don't you people have proofreaders at your shops? Or spell check? Or high school English teachers looking to earn a little tax-free money under the table? If an advertisement is for hamburger's, book's, dvd's, etc; I will not patronize that establishment. And most likely, I will have to reroute my entire trip to avoid driving past it.

«·»

Dear Karma,

I don't actually think that making me "sitting-on-the-toilet-puking-into-the-trash-can" sick is an equitable payback for my calling Harry Reid a "douche".

«·»

Dear Gloria Steinem & Betty Friedan,

While I appreciate your intention to make sure that I grow up in a world where women are valued equally, I find myself longing for the days of full-service gas stations. I had to pump my own gas in the freezing cold this morning. I much prefer the old way; when a nice young man would fill a lady's fuel tank while she sat primly in her nice, warm vehicle. Also, as I was leaving Quiktrip this morning, instead of holding the door open when I *clearly* had both hands full, a perfectly capable young man let it hit me in the forehead, then some other guy nearly killed us both trying to make sure I didn't change lanes in front of him. Chivalry *is* dead. And so was I, almost.

《·》

Dear Stephen King,

While your book *Under the Dome* is really great, I am finding it difficult to read a 1,100 page HARDCOVER book in bed, in the bathtub, and especially in a tanning bed. I have dropped it on my foot twice and my face once. Might I suggest a collection of smaller volumes next time around?

《·》

Dear Girl Scouts of America,

I am convinced that Girl Scouts are actually evil little trolls whose goal is to make people fat. They camp out in front of Wal-Mart like little crack dealers hanging out on urban street corners. The Thin Mints are my favorite.

《·》

Dear National Retailers,

You can stop sending me emails about your Black Friday Sales now. There exists nothing on Earth which can be purchased with money that I would get up early and fight hordes of other humans for a bargain on. I will, in fact, be happy to pay double for your products in order to avoid the crazies.

«·»

Dear Craigslist Rules Department,

I seriously wonder what kind of logic makes it OK for people to post pictures of their genitals on Craigslist, but my posting to give away for free a set of twin mattresses was removed as an illegal posting. Seriously? I can show people my hoo-hah but I can't give my kids' mattresses to a good home?

«·»

Dear My Extended Family,

When I die, could y'all please make sure that my obituary tells people what actually happened in the moments preceding my demise? They never tell the details, and unless the deceased is really old, it makes me wonder if it was something contagious of which I should be aware. Even if I am a 'Darwin Award' contender and something sad but really kind of funny happened to me or I came down with some rare medical thing that people might want to Google, just tell it like it is. Or was.

«·»

Dear Wal-Mart,

Obviously the person within your organization who authorized the decision to repaint the Sand Springs Wal-Mart Supercenter brown instead of blue does not have an autistic child. We are now thirty minutes into our third nervous breakdown about why "THE OLD WAL-MART NEEDS TO COME BACK!"

«·»

Dear People Who Hike for Fun,

I've just read yet another news story about missing hikers. Hiking is a very dangerous hobby, apparently. You never read much about missing cross-stitchers or missing stamp collectors. As a non-hiker, I am feeling pretty superior with my 'Things I Do for Fun' choices just about now.

《·》

Dear U.S. Postal Service,

Might I suggest that the United States Postal Service would not be losing billions (billions? Seriously?) of dollars a year if you guys could actually deliver stuff on time and if my mail lady wasn't such a bitch.

《·》

Dear Lego Corporation,

Whomever decided to change 'Legos' from a big box full of rectangles that kids turned into stuff with their imagination, to 100 million pieces that are all different shapes (and which take the kids' moms all day to put together and ten minutes for the kids to lose the pieces and scatter them all over the damn house) sets that you now sell, sucks and should be fired. Or executed.

《·》

Dear Transportation Safety Administration,

Do breast implants show up on those new full-body scanners at the airport? If so, can I get a free mammogram next time I travel?

《·》

Dear e-Harmony,

I don't actually need another husband, no matter how many "degrees of compatible" you think I am with the charming and eligible bachelors you keep trying to hook me up with. Kenny and I are *zero* degrees of compatible and we have been married for fifteen years, so please quit spamming me.

《·》

Dear Straight Men,

The reason we are interested in the Royal Wedding is that our mothers started reading us fairy tales when we were lap babies. Every little girl dreams of being the ordinary girl marrying the handsome prince. So, if you ever want to get laid again stop making fun of us. It is bad enough that we are stuck with you instead of our own personal prince.

Sincerely,

The people with ovaries and the gay men

《·》

Dear Next Door Man Who Woke My Whole Family Up with Your Stupid Weed-Eater at 7 A.M. today,

I am sorry that Scarlett is outside barking her fool head off at 11 P.M. I will bring her in for the night just as soon as I'm done being a vindictive bitch.

《·》

Dear Mark Zuckerberg,

There really should be a Facebook Rule that says if you give birth to someone, they are not allowed to "un-friend" you every time you piss them off.

《·》

Dear iPhone Autocorrect,

Thanks so much for texting my husband at work to tell him that I had Tina ready for lunch. I was actually trying to offer tuna.

《·》

Dear Wal-Mart Shoppers,

I know that when I drive by the front doors of the store I am obligated to yield to pedestrians, but if you are walking out of the store you have a responsibility to pull your head out of your ass and make sure there isn't a car *right in front* of you! I swear, it's like people are trying to get hit by a slow-moving car so they can sit on their butts and collect disability checks. It isn't a game of *Frogger*, people.

《·》

Dear People Who Are Losing Their Damn Minds Because Hostess Went Bankrupt,

May I politely point out- Twinkies are not even all that delicious.

《·》

Dear People of North Sand Springs,

Just in case you heard what sounded like a murder-in-progress tonight, don't be alarmed! I was just cutting Marshall's toenails. Autistic people aren't big on people with sharp objects invading their personal space.

《·》

Dear Old Men with This New Thing Called 'Low T',

If your testosterone levels are so low that you need to take that underarm testosterone replacement medicine where the commercial says you should not let your armpits come into contact with pregnant women or children, and it could cause you to go blind, have a heart attack, stroke, or just plain old drop dead- then God is trying to tell you that you need to forget getting laid and get a new hobby. Just sayin'.

《·》

Dear Teenage Girls at the Junior High,

Wearing shorts with UGG boots does not make you look cute and ready for autumn. It makes you look like a Special Ed kid whose mom didn't have the energy to fight with you before you left the house this morning.

《·》

Dear Fellow Wal-Mart Shoppers,

I am very sorry that my special needs son peeing his pants while he was sitting in the back of a cart was so disturbing to you all. I personally think that the lady in line in front of me who loaded an entire cart full of groceries onto the conveyor belt with one hand while she ate an *entire* deli container of fried chicken

117

livers with the other hand was way more of freak show. But maybe that's just me.

《·》

Dear People Who Live On My Street,

Although you might have feared that your lives were in imminent danger this morning due to the loud screaming and wild gesticulating coming from my front yard, rest assured- I was neither fending off a masked intruder nor disarming an explosive device. I was trying to keep my autistic teenage son from eating the yellow gummy bear that has been on the driveway for almost a week.

《·》

Dear Karma,

Thanks. I owe you one! I can't tell you how happy I was when the lady with the apparently perfect toddler in line behind me at Reasor's (and who was shaking her head at Marshall's "I'm happy to be in the checkout line at Reasor's" dance) was parked next to me in the parking lot. While my son was quietly sitting in the car while I unloaded my cart, *hers* was throwing himself to the pavement screaming like a banshee because he didn't want to get into his car seat. Yes, I did smile at her so she would also appreciate the delicious irony.

Chapter 13

There's already been an attempted murder and it's not even 10 am...

I just broke up a fight between my sons. The good thing about autistic kids is they rarely fight because, honestly, they just don't give a shit about what other people are doing enough to get pissed.

After it was over:

Me: "It's going to be a long day, Elizabeth."

Liz: "Yep. There's already been an attempted murder and it's not even 10 A.M."

*****

This is an actual conversation that took place in my kitchen this morning:

Carter: "MOM, why are you speaking bird?"

Me: "Huh?"

Carter: "You were speaking bird. I just heard you."

Me: "It is actually called whistling."

*****

I seriously need a vacation from my life. Today my two most uttered phrases have been "let go of your pee-wee" and "do *not* sneeze in my hair".

*****

Me: (asleep)

Carter (tap, tap, taps on my forehead): "Mom, MOM! Wake up!"

Me: "WHAT?!?"

Carter: "You have a zit. Wake up and pop it."

Can someone please remind me why we needed another baby?

****

Drive somewhere with a pack of teenagers and you too can hear fine music with such classic lyrics as *'they buy me Gucci 'cause they want my coochie'.*

*****

Why do all little kids missing teeth look like tiny hillbillies?

*****

So. We had all five of the kids at Olive Garden for my birthday:

Carter (eating salad): "Ow!"

Hayley: "What?"

Carter: "This thing tastes like... electricity!"

Me: "It's an onion."

Carter: "It tastes like electricity."

Kenny: "How do you know what *electricity* tastes like?"

*****

Me: "Since dad isn't home tonight- I am not cooking. What do you want for dinner?"

Carter: "Croutons."

Me: "You can't have just croutons. How about a *salad* with croutons?"

Carter: "Ok. I will just pick the salad out of it."

*****

I am currently refereeing a shouting match about whether or not the movie is called *"Snow White and the Seven Drawers"*.

*****

Carter has just informed me that he wants to hunt Easter eggs with candy inside, *not* Easter eggs with eggs inside.

*****

Carter: "What time are Grammie and Papaw coming to our house?"

Me: "Five o'clock. Why? Are you excited about hunting Easter eggs when they get here?"

Carter: "No, I want to watch Papaw take his dentures out."

*****

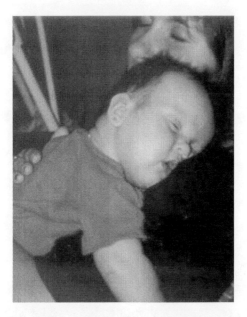

If I could pick a single moment in my life to go back to, not to change but just to enjoy again, this would be it. This is my middle daughter Hayley.

She had severe colic for six straight months, so holding her while she was peaceful was a rare and precious gift.

*****

Me: "Elizabeth, go help Marshall with the TV."

Liz: "Ok, but it's not gonna work!"

Me: "Huh?"

Liz: "He wants to watch a video and the VCR isn't working."

Me: "What's wrong with the VCR?"

Liz: "There's a pretzel in it."

Me: "Well of course there is."

*****

We are doing 'Last Day of School' teacher's gifts tonight. I give Carter a plain bag and markers and tell him to decorate the bag for his teacher's present. This. Is not exactly what I had in mind.

*****

Sleepover math: 4 thirteen-year-olds = 13 four-year-olds.

*****

Carter: "What happened to my underwear?"

Me: "I accidentally got them in with red clothes in the laundry and they turned pink, but I will bleach them and turn them back to white."

Carter: "NO! You can't do that!"

Me: "Why not?"

Carter: "Because they are beautiful."

*****

I call this one "Reason I Took a Really Quick Bath" or

"Oh Yeah, Well No One Wants to See You Naked Either."

*****

I am now referring an MMA fight that started over whether or not the movie we are about to see is called *"Putz in Boots"*.

*****

Me: "Marshall and I are going out to swim!"

Carter: "I'm going to stay inside and make some more evil minions."

*****

Me: "Carter! Turn! That! Computer! DOWN!!!"

Carter: "Why? Because you can't even hear yourself think?"

Me: "Um… yeah!"

Carter: "Maybe you should THINK louder!"

Me (thinking): "If school doesn't start soon, I am going to jail."

*****

1) Wins First Place for the Public Speaking portion in her Division at the FCCLA Regional Competition.

2) Squirts Hand Sanitizer in her eye.

*****

Carter (mumbling to himself): "You are not sick and you don't have a beaver."

Me: "What game are you playing on that computer *anyway*?"

*****

I slept on the floor last night and my hair smells like puke this morning. Being a mom with a sick kid is not unlike being a college freshman.

*****

Carter: "What does S.A.T.A.M stand for?"

Me: "Huh? What's it from?"

Carter: "Sonic the Hedgehog."

Me: "I have no earthly idea!"

Carter: "Huh?"

Me: "I do not know..."

Carter: "How can you not know?"

Me: "Because I don't actually know everything!"

Carter (sadly): "Oh. Is it because your brain is the size of a chicken nugget?"

Chapter 14

All my shoes suck...

Yes, as a matter of fact, every thought that comes into my head does have to go on Facebook. It's called 'Narcissistic Personality Disorder'. Look it up.

Things I have learned in my very first hour on Pinterest:

1) It's like Facebook, only without all the annoying men.

2) There are *lots* of ways to make cupcakes.

3) All my shoes suck.

4) I am not spending *nearly* enough time fixing my hair.

———————

I heard an ad this morning on the radio for a home security system. It made me think. I would feel so sorry for someone who decided to break into my house. They would go to all that trouble to get inside and then say to themselves: "*Where* are all the valuables?" (They are at school) "Do these people seriously not have *any* real jewelry?" (No) "Is there even *one* computer in this whole damn house that works correctly?" (No) "*Why* are there so many f&*%ing CATS?"

———————

I remember when saying "I am *not* going to be able to walk tomorrow" meant something other than "because I painted the kitchen ceiling today".

———————

Just drank chamomile tea for the first time. Now the inside of my mouth tastes like... I don't even know what... butterfly farts? Ew.

———————

So, you know how you start a minor bathroom cleaning project and the next thing you know your toilet is in the bathtub and your husband is sawing the plywood under-floor out?

———————

Does anyone by any chance know if eyelashes grow back? In *totally* unrelated news, I bought an at-home eyebrow waxing kit today.

———————

Today, I very narrowly missed my car getting t-boned by a hearse pulling out of a funeral home. I don't particularly want to die, but what an hysterical obituary that would've made!

———————

After months of searching, I have finally found the perfect new purse. It's the exact color and size I wanted. I am now ready to take over the world!

———————

About twice a year I clean my ring set. It is my platinum engagement ring, welded to Kenny's late mom's gold wedding band. I can't get them off anymore, so they get pretty dirty. It makes me very happy when they are clean, and very proud to have over 55 years of married on my hand.

Why is it that whenever I hear a helicopter flying over my house, I automatically assume that it's a police helicopter with a spotlight searching for a serial killer who is in my yard attempting to break into my house?

Cleaning out my purse before we head to the zoo for the day. I dumped it out onto the bed and it looks like the debris field from a miniature airplane crash.

I had a dream last night that I woke up in an asylum for neurotic children and animals. Then I realized I wasn't asleep.

Definition of the word 'dilemma': Dropping your favorite $6 pair of sunglasses into the toilet at Walgreen's.

Liz: "Why aren't you wearing your Wonder Woman tiara?"

Me: "Because I am laying down."

Liz: "But it's your source of power. Now you're just a regular mom."

I am going to have to find a different route to take my kids to school next year. Someone built a new house this summer and bought a very nice giant rock that is engraved with their family name. It contains a completely unnecessary apostrophe.

Advice I gave to my daughter with the waist-length hair as she started her freshman year: "You have *got* to start wearing makeup or everyone's going to think you are a Pentecostal."

I was just thinking to myself that the reason I am glad it's a snow day tomorrow isn't because I want my kids home all day (because I don't), but because I don't want to drive to three different schools and back in the cold. Then I thought to myself "there should be some kind of delivery service where you could get someone else to take your kids for you". Then it dawned on me that they already have that- it's called a school bus and if I weren't so neurotic and overprotective I would let them ride it. Then I decided to just quit thinking.

The mystery of why my call-in Chinese food wasn't ready when I arrived at 'Lin Cuisine' was solved when I was back at home eating my food and 'China Star' called to see why I never picked up my order.

Liz: "You know how people teach babies to talk by making animal sounds like 'a cow says moo'? Do foreign people make the same words or is it different in their own language?"

Me: "I think the 'moo' is just the sound the cow makes so it would be the same no matter the language, but you should Google it."

Liz: "What do I type in?"

Me: "What you just asked me..."

Liz: "Isn't that kind of long?"

Yep, this is what people whose kids don't play sports do on the weekends.

I went jeans shopping today. Tried on 17 pairs, bought 1. I need a sedative now.

———————

Today I cleaned out my DVR and my email inbox. It was hard work, and I am exhausted.

———————

You can see the little white pool floaty in my above-ground pool in the satellite photo of my house on Google Earth. This is *beyond* disturbing.

———————

I was talking to someone recently about my best girl friend from college. They asked if I was still in touch with her and I said "Nope. I haven't talked to her in years. Actually not since I married her boyfriend." My advice: Be loyal to your friends, ladies. Don't steal their men. If I had taken this advice, I could've saved myself over $10,000 in attorney's fees.

———————

Me: (sitting on my bed watching I.D. and hiding from my children)

Carter: "What are you doing up here?"

Me: "Watching non-Veggie Tales tv..."

Carter: "Can I sit on the bed with you?"

Me: "Yep, but you'll have to change the channel."

Carter: "Because I'm not allowed to watch I.D.?"

Me: "Yep, it's not for kids."

Carter: (scrolling through the DVR for a kids' movie)

Television (still on I.D.): "Joy didn't run off with another man like he said- Joy... was. Dead."

Carter: "Who's Joy?"

Me: "The lady on the show."

Carter: "What happened to her?"

Me: "Her husband killed her."

Carter: "Oh. Is she R.I.P.?"

Me: "Huh?"

Carter: "Rest in Peace-ing?"

Me: "It's Resting in Peace. Can you hurry up and change the channel please?"

Carter: "Are you going to take a nap now?"

Me: "Yes. You're wearing me out."

Carter: "Can I watch I.D.?"

Me: "No."

I really should have paid more attention to the birth control chapter in health class.

I've never been jealous of my only sister. We are far enough apart in age and have different enough interests that we complement each other really well. But I swear to gawd I am coveting her tank-less hot water system. No matter when - 6am, 11am, 2:34pm, 7pm, 12am- I decide to get into the shower there's always someone else taking a shower. It's like the 'Murphy's Law' of plumbing.

I think that instead of always wondering what kind of wine pairs with which food, I will just be honest and try to figure out which *food* goes with whichever wine is in my glass at the time.

———————

Liz: "Did you know that there are Miley Cyrus and Robin Thicke Halloween costumes this year?"

Me: "No. Does the ass of the Miley one Velcro onto the crotch of the Robin one?"

———————

Men: "I don't understand why you are so excited about William & Kate's new baby."

Women: "Because she married a real live PRINCE and turned into an actual PRINCESS and had a teeny PRINCE baby and ever since we were little girls that has been our most favorite dream. So *that* is why we care. If you don't like it, take it up with Walt Disney."

Chapter 15

Give the guy a fish...

If you give a man a fish, you will feed him for a day. If you teach a man to fish, you won't have to put up with him for 10 months out of the year because he will go fishing whenever the weather is even moderately tolerable so you can hang out at home in your pajamas and eat Captain Crunch for dinner and no one will bitch...

Women take pictures strategically to make things appear smaller. Men do the opposite. This is Kenny- my favorite husband.

~~~~~

Why is it that if a husband asks his wife what she wants for her birthday, she can come up with hundreds of things, depending on how much money he has, what time of year it is, and where he will be shopping. If a wife asks her husband what he wants for his birthday, he will give her the "hubba-hubba" eyes. Every. Single. Time.

~~~~~

Is it just me, or are the 'Extenze' and 'Viagra' commercials with the creepy old guys making sexy eyebrows and laughing about how they are fixing to get laid the yickiest things ever?

~~~~~

If "the enemy of my enemy is my friend", what does that make the second ex-wife of my ex-husband?

~~~~~

My husband is getting up at 4 A.M. tomorrow to go fishing. He fished until 1 A.M. last night. The only reason I would ever fish at these ungodly hours is if my family were starving to death. Nope. Not even then.

~~~~~

I just read that a former NFL player was arrested for "patronizing a prostitute." It took me a full minute to realize that it meant he was being a client of the hooker, not that he was treating her in a condescending manner.

~~~~~

My husband is convinced that I am trying to kill him, which is a ridiculous idea. I mean, he is still alive, right?

~~~~~

Today, I am again thankful that I was born without a penis. Those things sure do cause a lot of trouble. The news is full of stories of them wandering away from home and having misadventures. If you have one, it's a full time job to take care of it. What with all the touching, readjusting, and worrying about it. You can't manage to pee *in* a freaking toilet with one. If it suddenly stops working, you have to take medicine with some of the most horrifying side effects. Plus, if I had one I probably wouldn't be so in love with the *Twilight* movies.

~~~~~

Referring to Keith Urban fans as "wet-pantied freaks" is not a good way to get yourself laid at my house. True story.

~~~~~

My husband and I are rarely in the same vehicle at the same time (which is the secret to our marriage lasting). He is driving and just asked me how fast my new car will go. This is a trick question.

~~~~~

Let it be known that on October eighteenth, in the year of our Lord two-thousand and eleven, Kenny and Tami Tate agreed on something. Neither party verbally beat the other into submission, no one was just trying to be nice (or get lucky), and there was no week-long debate beforehand.

~~~~~

The most romantic part of the date? When the 'Date-Mobile' is *your* car and he sees that you're below ¼ tank of gas so he stops and fills it up for you. And he pays. *And* he skips the lecture about how "You Should Never Let Your Gas Tank Get Under Half Full".

~~~~~

I'm always finding business cards that women have slipped to my husband lying on his bathroom counter. But since he is a Realtor and it means they are showing his listings, I am ok with it.

~~~~~

My husband came home with a present he bought for me today. It is a pumpkin cupcake with cream cheese icing from a little bakery in our town. Gentlemen; *this* is how it is done!

~~~~~

Things I have observed while spending the evening in front of the TV with my husband:

1) Football games are really long if you watch the whole thing instead of just the highlights.

2) Our TV is some fancy new kind where the people on the screen can hear us if we shout at them, apparently.

3) Jesus is not as interested in football as I was led to believe.

~~~~~

This weekend I had the pleasure of sharing a porch conversation with two very manly men. They were swapping "Goriest Emergency Room Visit" stories. I patiently listened to a full recap of two fishing hook removals, one poisonous spider bite, and one plantar wart cutting. Then, I politely asked if it was my turn and launched into my own personal three anesthesia-less vaginal deliveries with and without episiotomies, and two C-sections (one with a failed epidural and subsequent 'blood patch' procedure). Whomever said women aren't tougher than men- never worked in Labor & Delivery. I win.

~~~~~

Me: "Carter, QUIT messing with your junk! If it's bothering you, go to the bathroom to adjust it."

Carter: "It's NOT junk and it's not bothering anyone! I am just straightening it all out."

~~~~~

Things not to say to the mother of your children (and the only woman you're technically allowed to have sex with): "Be glad *you're* not the one taking the life insurance physical. *You* wouldn't pass."

~~~~~

I washed and vacuumed my car yesterday and, because it smelled like Sonic and dirty children, I sprayed it with that cherry air freshener they have at the car wash. I haven't used that stuff in decades. My car now smells exactly like every awkward first date I ever had as a teenager. Throw in some Polo or Drakkar cologne, and it would be uncanny.

~~~~~

I thought there was a meth lab in my basement. Turns out it was just my husband making fishing lures.

~~~~~

Things I have learned from watching the epic miniseries *'The Bible'*: every time things are going along swimmingly, some guy gets goo-goo eyes for a chick and it all turns to crap.

~~~~~

I am pretty proud of myself. I was just about to pour a heaping capful of extra-scenty fabric softener into the washer with my husband's Gore-Tex fishing suit. Then it hit me...

~~~~~

Incredibly exciting news at the Tate house this weekend!!! Kenny had a giant dumpster delivered to the driveway! We can throw away all *kinds* of junk and chop down and throw away all our trees!!!

Chapter 16

Will you marry me?

My youngest son is the baby of the family and is very affectionate and very unaware of the term "personal space". I was having a serious conversation with him today about how to hug a lady - without copping a feel. I told him that the only time a boy is allowed to touch a girl's boobs is if he is married to her. He took a minute, thought it over, and then very seriously and earnestly asked me to marry him.

One of my "gifted" daughters has five cuts on the top of her foot. I'll give you three guesses how they got there. Never mind, you'll never guess. The *ceiling fan* in her bedroom. She. Cut. Her. Foot. On. The. Ceiling. Fan. Laying on the bunk-bed talking on the cell phone with her feet on the ceiling. Dear Lord, *please* help me to remember this day the next time she puts her hand on her hip and informs me how much smarter than me she is.

*****

I find it very ironic that someone I used to breastfeed freaks out when I ask her to share a drink with me at the movies.

*****

Me: (barely awake and headed to pee)

Carter: "Can I have a Reasor's bag?"

Me (assuming he needed a paper sack for some kind of craft project): "Yeah."

Me (Returning to my bedroom later-just in time to see my son jump off my bed with a plastic bag hooked on to his shoulders like a back pack): "OHMYGAWD! What are you DOING?"

Carter: "Parachuting."

Me: "Well, don't jump off anything higher than the bed."

*****

I love it when this happens: Five minutes before dinner is on the table and my child says "MOM! I totally forgot to tell you when you picked me up from school, but I have to have some things for science class tomorrow- for a grade. But it's ordinary stuff we probably already have. I need vinegar, a 2-liter bottle, brown clay, and a box of baking soda."

*****

Rain Man goes to the petting zoo:

Me: "Don't pull the llama's ear."

Marshall: "Ok."

Me: "Don't pull the llama's ear."

Marshall: "Ok."

Me: "Don't pull the llama's ear."

Marshall: "Ok."

Me: "If that freaking llama bites you, you'd better not cry about it!"

Marshall: "Ok."

Me: "Marshall, LET GO!"

Marshall: "Ok...OW!"

*****

This is what my daughter just said to me. Let me rephrase that. This is what my daughter just had the *balls* to say to me: "I'm just letting you know that since I overslept by 30 minutes and you didn't bother to wake me up, we are going to be 30 minutes late leaving for school." Oh, really? I beg to differ.

*****

Actual dinner conversation (ironically, at a Mexican restaurant)

Hayley: "Guess what? I have a 105 in Spanish Class!"

Me: "Awesome! How do you say '105' in Spanish?"

Hayley: "I dunno, I'm not really good with the Spanish numbers."

*****

These are my older daughters- as toddlers and now. Kiernan seriously wanted to be an only child...

*****

My auto correct knows the word Kardashian. I should probably just kill myself now.

*****

Liz just heard Bon Jovi singing *'It's My Life'* and said "Why are those old guys screwing up a Glee song?"

*****

I am going to take up smoking. At the age of 42. That way I can have an excuse to sit on my front porch for ten minutes every hour without my kids like my neighbors do. And also I will lose weight.

*****

I walked into the living room this morning to turn on the lights. This. Is how I found Woody and Jessie. Apparently Toy Story 4 is gonna be a porno.

*****

I have recently come to the realization that holding your newly-born child in your arms for the first time is not nearly as awe-inspiring and terrifying as riding in a car being driven by your newly-permitted child for the first time.

*****

That damn crying baby in *'The Godfather'* is the most irritating human in the history of humans. It's Sonny Corleone's child and the mom carries it into every scene in the old man's house screaming its face off. Someone should make it an offer it can't refuse.

*****

Why does it take my daughters longer to get ready for school than it took me to get ready for my first wedding?

*****

Whomever said "there is no such thing as a stupid question" has never met any of my children.

*****

Is this transcript too long to print in her obituary?

Liz: "I *can't* feed the dogs- I'm wearing a dress!"

Me: "Put on some sweats."

Liz: "I can't find my sweats, can you help me look?"

Me (digging through the piles of clothes on her closet floor): "I don't see them, just put on some jeans."

Liz: "I don't want to wear jeans. I want pajama pants, which I can't find either."

Me: "What do you want *me* to do about it? I already helped you look."

Liz: "How about you do some *laundry*?"

*****

So, I just taught Elizabeth how to shave her legs for the first time by shaving them for her. I cut her shinbone from the foot all the way up to the knee...

*****

Took the kids to the zoo today. We had a run-in with "Will: Tram Safety Advisor." I kid you not, that was his title. He had a badge and everything.

*****

I thought it might be fun to take the scenic route home over the gently rolling hills. I was incorrect.

*****

Just left Sonic Drive-In. The teenage girl 'Car-Hops' are all in Halloween costumes. Apparently the only available choices were: Slutty Pocahontas, Slutty Eskimo, Slutty Alice-In-Wonderland, and Strip Club Kitty Cat. I guess those little change holders they wear on their belts will come in handy in their future endeavors.

*****

Liz: "Why are you laying down? It's afternoon!"

Me: "Because for some stupid reason, I haven't been able to sleep at night this whole week!"

Liz: "Why don't you sleep at night?"

Me: "I wish I knew, because this sure sucks."

Elizabeth K. Tate, M.D.: "It sounds like you might have insomnia."

*****

Or, however your kids play in the snow...

*****

Carter got his uniform for Special Olympics softball today. Of *course* he is number 13.

*****

Halloween: Time to let my kids go beg for candy at the doors of people in our neighborhood whom we never talk to the other 364 days of the year.

*****

Things that sum up my family- Thanksgiving Day: Hayley shot a deer this morning. Kiernan made a Tofurkey.

*****

I'd like to extend my apologies to everyone in the balcony who took Communion after us this morning, since Carter felt the need to touch 5 or 6 squares of bread before he chose the perfect one.

*****

This morning, I had an epiphany as I was walking Marshall into his Special Ed class. I was thinking about how much work it is helping him get dressed, brushing his teeth for him, washing his face, checking his hands, making sure he peed, cleaning the pee off the floor because he cannot aim, packing his lunch, finding his jacket, putting his shoes on and tying them for him, etc. He requires as much personal hygiene help as a three-year-old. Even the things he takes care of himself require a second opinion.

I am starting to accept the fact that he will live at home as an adult and will still require a lot of care, but I was feeling jealous of everyone with "normal" teenagers. And THEN. IT. HIT. ME. Every morning I dodge Elizabeth as she is getting herself ready for school. She has a lot of hair and it requires a lot of intervention. She lays waste to her bedroom every single day just by picking out her own clothes and dressing herself. She has really bad PMS. I have to purchase feminine hygiene products (often in a special trip to the store late at night because I don't use them myself so unless she tells me, I don't know she's about to run out of them). I am forever waiting in the car in the morning while she does one last thing. My epiphany is- I am SO VERY THANKFUL that my autistic kid is not a girl! Sooooo thankful. So. Very. Thank. Full.

Chapter 17

They are just waiting to eat my hair...

Dogs want to be your friend because they love you and it makes them happy to be in your presence. Cats want to be your friend so that when you fall asleep they can chew off your hair.

5:58 am-Carter: "Mummble, mummble, mumm mumm..."

Me (stumbles into his room and asks): "What now?"

Carter: "Tick was licking my eye."

Me: "Go back to sleep."

Carter: (goes instantly back to sleep)

Me (thinking): "How in the heck do you fall back asleep after a cat licks you in the eyeball? I may never sleep again and it wasn't even *my* eye!"

𝄞 𝄞 𝄞

I hate it when you throw a cat off your bed in the middle of the night. And it lands on a sleeping dog.

𝄞 𝄞 𝄞

Milk. Bitch will cut you for it.

§ § §

I think I am one cat away from being that house where people drive by and drop off unwanted cats.

§ § §

How I almost died today: 7 A.M.- My dogs are raising holy Hades in the back yard. Scarlett's jumping and is about to hang herself on the privacy fence. I peek out and see a fluffy little white dog scratching at the fence. I go outside, around the house and lock eyes with the *pitbull* who is with her. He runs at me and I haul ass back into my house and shut the glass door just as he runs head first into it. The only reason I out-ran him is that the six feet of chain he is dragging slowed him down. He probably was friendly and just wanted me to pet him, but still.

§ § §

Me: "I know you don't like to get your paws wet. You should've left the kitchen before I started mopping it..."

Tuck: "meoooww"

Me: "Looks like you are gonna be sitting there for quite a while."

Tuck: "meeee-ow"

Me: "Sucks to be you."

Tuck: "mmmmm-oooowwowowow."

ৡ ৡ ৡ

If you want to freak your kids out- reset a cat's broken tail without a veterinary degree.

ৡ ৡ ৡ

So, I had to give the kittens their first bath this morning. Does anyone have the number of a reputable plastic surgeon?

$$\text{\textit{\&}\,\textit{\&}\,\textit{\&}}$$

Korra, my grand-kitten, is very special. I just want to take a Sharpie and make the orange half of her face match the black half!

$$\text{\textit{\&}\,\textit{\&}\,\textit{\&}}$$

Is it bad that I occasionally want to make Tock watch that abused animal commercial with the sad cats and dogs so that he can see how good he has it and adjust his attitude accordingly?

$$\text{\textit{\&}\,\textit{\&}\,\textit{\&}}$$

I hate monkeys. They are like creepy old people who can't talk.

§ § §

Me: "Carter! What on Earth is all the ruckus about?"

Carter: "Hag won't quit trying to lay down on me!"

Me: "Well snap your fingers and tell him to GO! LAY! DOWN!"

Carter: "I cannot."

Me: "Why not?"

Carter: "Because my fingers are not *sharp* enough for snapping!"

§ § §

You know how in an urban setting, society begins to break down within days after a disruption in the supply chain of food and other goods? Apparently that time frame is slightly accelerated in the feline population.

We have been out of cat food for exactly twenty minutes and all of my cats are alternately crying mournfully, racing around the house like aimless bats out of hell, pawing at the doors and

155

windows in a desperate attempt to search for food outside, and generally being insane pains in the ass.

$$\text{\$ \$ \$}$$

One thing you really don't want to hear your child say: "MOM! This kitten is going to need more oxygen!"

$$\text{\$ \$ \$}$$

If anyone needs a crime committed today, give me a call. I was putting claw covers on a "reluctant" cat earlier and my fingertips are so covered in nail glue that I no longer have fingerprints.

$$\text{\$ \$ \$}$$

Me: (Mopping the living room floor this morning)

Liz: "WHY are you mopping the floor right now?"

Me: "Because the dog peed on it!"

Liz: "How do you know it was the dog?"

Me: "Because of the location, smell, splatter pattern, and size of the paw prints. I am pretty much just like a CSI- but for pets."

$$\text{\$ \$ \$}$$

I was going to ask "why do my cats all freak out and start meowing at me when their food bowls get half empty?" But then it dawned on me that when my refrigerator gets half empty I get in the car and drive to the grocery store.

$$\text{\$ \$ \$}$$

R.I.P. Larry the Goldfish that Carter won at the fair last month. Tuck fished him out of the aquarium and played with him on the kitchen floor until he was a little piece of fish jerky while we were asleep last night. Guess it's time to buy a cover for the tank.

§ § §

Math for potential cat owners:

I have 1 cat= "Oh, this is just like being a mom. I can totally handle this. She is so cute and smart and I am doing such a good job."

I have 2 cats= "I have lost complete control of my entire life. I am a failure and should never have kids."

I have 3 or more cats= "I am not even qualified to take care of myself, much less another living creature."

§ § §

Picture this: I'm walking and ducking and shooting a plastic-pellet pistol (urban warfare style) at 11 P.M. Trying to get the damn stray cat mating ritual to move to someone else's porch. Since the crafty stud cat is staying just out of the pellet's reach, I've gone halfway up the street and then halfway down the other side stealthily shooting and reloading. As I'm giving up and am almost home, my across-the-street neighbor, to whom I've never actually been formally introduced, lets out a low chuckle. He's been standing next to his car smoking this whole time. He tells me that someone really needs to do something about all these damn stray cats. HELLO- DIDN'T YOU JUST SEE ME GOING ALL RAMBO ON THEM?!? I am rarely at a loss for words and almost never get embarrassed, but I found myself being both. I bid him goodnight and walked normally (as normally as one can wearing clogs and carrying a pink plastic gun) back to my own house. Oh, and the stupid horny cats weren't even scared. They thought it was a game.

§ § §

I read that "Crazy Cat Lady" isn't just a descriptive term, but a new scientific theory. Apparently humans who contract toxoplasmosis from their cats can experience a change in their brains that makes them want to have more and more cats and that makes them immune to the smell of cat urine. Seems legit.

ยยย

We lost a really good family member today. Hag (short for Merle Haggard, of course...) outlived his owners, who just happened to be my husband's parents. He has been a great addition to our menagerie, but never really stopped being restless and seemed like he was always planning to find his way back to his real masters. It makes me happy to think that he has finally found them again. Old dogs...

ยยย

Chapter 18

This Baby is Ruining My Life...

I saw a tabloid in the grocery store line recently. It was a picture of a hugely pregnant reality star with swollen feet and a sad face. The headline was epic. *It read "This Baby is Ruining My Life!"... If she's this upset with the thing while it is still a fetus- what's she going to do when it grows up and starts blaming her for giving it a ridiculous name? The headline should've read "I'm Fixing to Ruin This Baby's Life!"*

Speaking of pregnancy, there was recently a Facebook game called "Tell 12 Interesting Things About Your Pregnancy". Here are mine:

1) I got pregnant.

2) I had a premature baby exactly 50 minutes after arriving at the hospital, and with no anesthesia. I had a very aggressive episiotomy and had a total of 72 internal and external stitches. I swore before God that I would never have another child.

3) I got pregnant.

4) I had a premature baby 15 minutes after I got to the hospital, again with no anesthesia. I swore to never let my husband touch me again as long as I lived.

5) That husband and I got a divorce. I met Kenny, renounced my chastity vow, turned up pregnant within 3 months, and had to renounce my "I'm never getting married ever again" vow.

6) I had a premature baby 17 hours after arriving at the hospital and had a little shot of Stadol to make me talk about inappropriate subjects while I was delivering a baby with no anesthesia.

7) I got pregnant while taking the 'Birth Control Pill That Is Safe to Take While Nursing a Baby' when said baby was 4 months old.

8) I had a premature baby via emergency C-section and had to have a blood patch when my epidural block leaked and it was the single most painful thing I have ever experienced and made me swear to never have another epidural or another baby.

9) I got pregnant. (Alcohol makes me violate my chastity vows.)

10) I had a premature baby via planned c-section and even though he was twice the size of the previous premature baby, he had the least developed lungs and had to stay in the NICU for twice as long. I had my tubes tied at the same time because I no longer trusted myself around alcohol or my husband's penis.

11) Three months later, and before the Tubal Ligation was paid for-my uterus fell out.

12) I am a super-hero.

———————

It is really unfair that people only stay babies for two years. As moms, we go through nine (ish) months of having our bodies possessed by tiny demons. Then, during the two years where the kid is actually cute and portable on the *outside* of us, we are so sleep deprived that we barely remember them. They stop being babies around the time they start talking and walking, which is when we start wishing for them to shut up and sit down already. Then we are stuck with sixteen years of having short, bossy people wrecking our homes and demanding to be fed and driven places. This is *such* a rip off.

I've learned that having babies does not make your boobs permanently bigger. Breast implants do.

———————

The only thing worse than hearing another person puke is hearing another person puke when they are sitting behind you in your car, and you are their mom, so you know you are going to have to be in charge of clean-up.

———————

Today I gave one of my autistic sons the Heimlich maneuver and performed at-home surgery to remove a rock embedded in the leg of the other. I am not a nurse and I am most definitely not getting paid enough for this.

———————

Is it wrong to sometimes secretly wish your husband will leave you so that you can have two weekends a month with no kids?

———————

According to Facebook, I was supposed to take cute photos of my kids with their Easter baskets and the whole adorable family in the front yard all dressed up for church. Seriously? Isn't it enough that I remembered to buy the dang candy and clothing?

———————

Some days, all you can do is laugh. And some days, all you can do is resist the urge to stick your head in the oven.

————————

As a mom, you spend a lot of years raising kids, which is a pretty thankless job. But every now and then you get a glimpse that all your hard work is paying off. Today I was mopping up spilled Kool-aid and managed to get a large chunk of broken pottery in the instep of my foot. As I'm hopping around trying not to scream bloody murder, Liz fetches me some Neosporin and a paper towel for the bleeding. Carter disappears and comes back and without saying a single word, picks up my foot, examines it closely, puts on a Band-aid, and then pats my arm. *Those* are the moments that make it worth all the years of pregnancy, nursing, cleaning up puke and poop (from places God never intended for it to be), sleepless nights, and endless worrying. I am raising empathetic, giving little people. All is well.

————————

I have a friend with a colicky newborn. Just the word 'colic' is enough to make me want to cry. Two of my kids had colic and it was *the hardest* thing I ever did in my whole career as a mom. Instead of having 5K runs to raise money to cure cancer, they should raise money to cure colic.

————————

Random Fact: The total birth weight of my all five of my kids is 29 pounds. The total amount of weight I gained in five shorter-than-average pregnancies is 295 pounds. This is *very* fuzzy math.

————————

I firmly believe that the best thing you can do for a group of grieving teenagers is to give them a place to be together and leave them alone to heal each other. Today I have seven of them in my house, one of whom found his mother dead in her bed of a heart attack yesterday. They are all piled on the floor like a litter of puppies. Hearing them laughing is the most wonderful sound in the world. No amount of sad words and sympathetic hugs from adult relatives will help this young man like the girls all holding him down and trying to put a bobby pin on his nipple will.

———————

Now that all but one of my kids is wearing adult-sized shoes, the pitter-patter of little feet down the hallway has been replaced with the heart-attack inducing sound of roving jack-booted para-military gangs of thugs storming my house.

———————

Yesterday, I took one of my kids to get braces, one of my kids got into a car wreck at college (ten hours away), one of my kids isn't speaking to me because I had the *audacity* to protest her posting bikini pics on Facebook, one of my kids was uncharacteristically pissy and hateful, and one of my kids threw up in his bed at 2 A.M. As I sat on the floor next to him silently willing him to go back to sleep and worrying about all five of them, it occurred to me that mothering is a *really* hard job.

———————

I had a movie date this evening! A cute guy kept sneakily trying to hold my hand in the dark. The movie was *'Alvin and the Chipmunks'*, and the boy's hand was very sticky and somewhat smallish. But still...

———————

I'm watching a documentary on Ireland, one of the *many* places I've never been. I am from a middle class Oklahoma family. Travel has not ever been a big part of my life. I plan to live long and prosperously enough to drink a piña colada on a tropical island, see the guards at Buckingham Palace, attend a Keith Urban concert in Australia, tour Washington D.C. in the spring, wear a Kimono in Japan, see the Eiffel Tower at night, visit New England in the fall, stand at Ground Zero in New York, spend a week at a dude ranch in New Mexico, get drunk at a California vineyard, buy a hand-woven basket on Nantucket, stroll the streets of Charleston in a white sundress and sandals, show off my boobs at Mardi Gras, and be terrified at the edge of the Grand Canyon. I'm over 40 now, so these things may not happen. But *more* than this, I hope that my kids will get to do all of these things. If I never leave Sand Springs, Oklahoma again; I hope my legacy of people will spread their wings and soar and do and see all of the wonderful things this world has to offer.

Things that make you cry so hard you can't breathe- when you get back home from the emergency room and your seriously injured child is in so much pain that he sits beside you, makes you promise not to touch his owies, cries into your shirt sleeve, and says "When I was falling why didn't you save me?"

In my grandmothers' generation, overwhelmed, exhausted, burnt-out women had "nervous breakdowns" and were sent to hospitals for a few weeks to recover, renew, and refresh. They really should have something like that today. We put way too much pressure on ourselves and each other. It is damaging our health and our souls, and is making us cranky and bitchy. We need to stand up for and help each other instead of competing with each other. Call one of your "mom friends" tonight and set up a lunch date. At a restaurant with a liquor license.

You would think that having teenage daughters and autistic sons would've taught me patience. Alas, it has simply made me want to constantly interrupt other people and say "Can we just skip all the bull-crap, cut to the chase, and move on to the next thing?"

If I had known how much fun baby kittens are when I was in my twenties, I never would've even had five babies. I would've just kept getting baby cats every year. Plus also, you can't leave baby people locked in the bathroom when you need to go somewhere.

Liz (complaining about a zit): "I won the genetic lottery. All the bad stuff I have I got from you."

Me (thinking to myself): "Well buckle up, sister. You ain't seen nothin' yet. Give it about 30 more years till all the *really* bad stuff kicks in."

"If you are having a sucky day, load up all your kids and go to Wal-Mart." - Said. No. One. Ever.

When a man asks you to sit on the porch and watch the sunset with him, you have to stop and do it. Especially if he is 10.

Does it make anyone else suspicious when people only post perfect pictures of themselves on Facebook and only talk about how wonderful/fantastic/amazing their spouse and kids are and how happy/healthy/blessed they are or is it just me who thinks "No way, dude"? Or does everyone else really not live with organized chaos like my entire life?

The good thing about having a lot of kids; when one of them breaks your heart, the others will cover it with Band-Aids.

I love Facebook. You can rekindle friendships, mend fences, and find something to laugh and cry about every day. You can dispense unsolicited medical, relationship, legal, political, and psychological advice- all while wearing your pajamas. You can carry on a conversation without having to lock yourself in the bathroom if the kids are running around like idiots. You can see what other people are having for dinner, what movies are good, and how fat your ex-husband's new girlfriend is. You can get on-the-spot weather updates with photos from people who don't even have a degree in meteorology, just an iPhone. You can get help finding your lost dog, help raising your kids, and help deciding if that spot on your arm looks like skin cancer. You can always find someone willing to take your side in whatever argument you are having with your irritating spouse. You can air your frustrations to a sympathetic audience. If someone pisses you off, you can delete them and not face prison time. You can follow friends' pregnancies, help them through crises, and wish them a happy birthday all without buying a stamp. You can post a hundred pics of yourself and zero of them will show how fat you've let your ass get.

If you can't remember something that happened in high school, at least two of your friends will. If you can't sleep, there will be at least four other people awake and online at any hour of the night. If there is a natural disaster and you have to live in a hotel or stay with relatives, you can keep in touch with all your friends and family and let them know you are still alive and sick of eating at McDonald's. If you need an expensive operation you can ask everyone for $10 and instantly have enough for that shiny new liver. You can show off your new tattoo without having to drop your shorts in public. If you are at a concert, you can see what the stage looks like from the other side of the stadium, because at least five of your friends are there posting pics instead of watching the show.

Everyone yearns for the 'Mayberry' days where everyone knew their neighbors by name and sat out on the front porch after supper waving at folks as they walked by. We can't get back to the "Good Old Days", but thanks to Facebook- we can have some pretty decent new ones...

Chapter 19

Did I hear that right?

When you have autistic kids, you just really never know what you are going to hear in any given day.

Carter has an auditory processing disorder that makes him have a hard time spitting out what he wants to say. I have a habit of filling in the words he's trying to think of for him to keep the conversation moving fast enough that he doesn't lose his train of thought. Sometimes it goes hilariously awry:

Me: "How was school today?

Carter: "I have a black eye."

Me (sees no evidence of a black eye, but decides to play along): "How did you get the black eye?"

Carter: "I was being an airplane and flying....and I fell into a.....chair....because I don't have...."

Me (prompting): "Wings?"

Carter: "No. Flying lessons."

?????

Maybe letting my youngest daughter (who just got her first pair of contacts today) practice removing them by letting her take mine out of my eyes was not the very *best* idea I've ever had.

?????

I just told my son to get his hand out of his pants, and that if he needed to touch his pee-wee he should go to the bathroom to do so. He literally *ran* to the bathroom. Boys are so gross.

?????

At four this morning, Carter woke me up by tapping my neck. Stop for a moment and imagine that you are dead asleep and someone taps you on your NECK!!! This child, in particular, is lucky I don't sleep with a gun. I say "WHAT?!?!?!?" He says "Do you want to give Tick a high-five?" Sometimes I think that I am the star of a secretly-filmed reality show that everyone knows about but me.

?????

Tonight I am in bed. Having a conversation via text message with my daughter. Not the one at college. The one in the living room.

?????

Paid $140 for 'Disney on Ice' tickets. Carter is spellbound. By the Zamboni.

?????

I just saw on my youngest daughter's Twitter feed exactly when and where she is going to be tonight. Said daughter is now deleting each and every Twitter 'follower' that is not a child in her grade at school. Her next oldest sister has been posting bikini pics of herself on Facebook. It's like there is contest to see who can get abducted by a pedophile first. I need a drink.

?????

Carter: "What happened to Icarus when he got too close to the sun?"

Me: "Who is Icarus?"

Carter: "From Icarus and Daedalus."

Me: "Is that from a show?"

Kenny: "No, it's from Greek Mythology."

Me (thinking): 'My life totally *is* a quiz show'.

?????

Who needs the gentle sounds of nature to wake you up when you can have a child sneeze all over your face and yell at you to wake up and get them a tissue at not quite 7 A.M. on spring break?

?????

I totally appreciate the sweet irony of watching my prematurely-born son struggling under the weight of the March of Dimes donation coin bank he filled this month and lugged into school today.

?????

Dumbo. Is on Netflix. The boys found it and just started it in the living room. I fled to my bedroom because that movie traumatized me so badly when I was a kid that I just can't even be in the same *room* with it.

?????

Words I did not expect to say today when I left the house this morning:

"OH MY GOD! STOP LICKING THAT BUFFALO'S NOSE!!!"

?????

Get ready to hand over that 'Mother of the Year' trophy. Today I took the kids to school. Marshall is the last one out of the car on the final stop of the morning. He climbs down out of the car and I look down and see that he is wearing black socks and *no shoes*! I will be doing the 'walk of shame' into the school office after I run home and grab him some shoes.

?????

So. I was arguing with Liz last night and told her that if she didn't stop talking I was going to take away her bedroom door for a week. She said *"You* can't take it off! And Dad is not here!" Today I used a screwdriver, a pair of pliers, and a hammer and took that smart-mouthed girl's bedroom door off all by myself. My mom will be so proud. She always said "One day you are going to have a daughter who acts just like you and I am going to sit back and laugh!" I have three. Thanks, Mom.

?????

I just very nearly decapitated my daughter this morning when she decided to check her face in the passenger-side door mirror on my Suburban. *After* she got out of the car and shut the door.

?????

Or, whatever YOU do at Mexican restaurants.

?????

There are two canisters on my kitchen counter. Only two.

Me: "What are you doing in there?"

Liz: "I'm putting sugar in my tea but I don't want this powdered sugar one."

Me: "Um, Dude. That's called flour."

?????

Elizabeth: "I think I might join the Debate Team next year. But I don't like the part where you have to wait for the other person to talk."

?????

7:08 am is *entirely* too early for the Macarena.

?????

Me: "So, what do you think?"

Carter: "About what?"

Me: "About my new hair. Do you like it short?"

Carter (typical man): "Nope."

Me: "Did you like it better long?"

Carter: "Yes."

Me: "When you grow up and get married, do you want your wife to have short hair or long hair?"

Carter: "Short."

Me: "Short hair? Really? Why?"

Carter: "Because you just got your hair made short and I'm going to marry you."

?????

At Redbox with a 'gifted' teenager today:

Liz: "Hey! It's like a vending machine, only with DVDs!"

Me: "It's exactly like a vending machine, only with DVDs."

?????

Me: "The direct withdrawal thingy for your braces is either jacked up this month or else they are finally paid for!"

Liz: "Cool! So does that mean I can get them off now?"

Me: "You still have baby teeth. You are gonna be in those things for at least two more years."

Liz: "This sucks."

Me (Thinking): "Yeah, you are welcome for the orthodontia that cost more than my car."

?????

What a coincidence! I was totally just thinking that I would love to stop right in the middle of blow drying my hair to take a picture of your hair with your phone so you can group text it to all your friends to see if you should wear it like that today or not.

?????

I walked into the kitchen to start dinner. Here is how I found the Evil Villain Jafar.

?????

Last night, Marshall was in the living room yelling dialogue from '*Toy Story*'. I'd had enough. Kenny said "Has it occurred to you that being sick all week and being stuck at home with you is driving him just as crazy as being stuck at home with him is driving you?" I had not considered this.

?????

Chapter 20

'Tis the season to be freaky...

Dear Santa: Listen up, you fat bastard... No Legos or toys with small parts this Christmas. I don't care how good the Tater Tots were this year!

Dear Santa, Jesus, and Karma,

   I seriously hope y'all were watching me today. I just spent an hour and sixteen minutes and $261 at Wal-Mart. I made it a special point to be nice, friendly, polite, and smiley to everyone, even the jerk in the camouflage suit who wouldn't let me past his giant self in the toy aisle. I also managed to be charitable in my thoughts of my fellow shoppers, even those whose "entitlements" my husband's hard earned money is paying for. Which was especially hard since the lady in line in front of me used W.I.C. vouchers for baby food and formula and she was wearing legit 'Miss Me' jeans and authentic new UGG boots which is total bullshit, but I hummed the song from the movie *'Frozen'* where Elsa builds the ice castle and tried to focus on that. I didn't even honk at the ass-hat who nearly ran me off the road in front of Arby's.

Love, Tami

* * *

If I *were* neurotic enough to put up Christmas decorations at my house before Thanksgiving, I would not just willy-nilly tell everyone on Facebook. I would keep that particular dirty secret to myself. Jeez, Louise people. One holiday at a time, please.

* * *

How I know it's almost Christmas: When one of my daughters compliments me on the "amazing job" I did. Cleaning the bathroom.

* * *

Christmas Vacation when I'm 19= Tequila shots and sleeping somewhere sketchy in yesterday's clothes. Christmas Vacation when I'm 39= NyQuil shots and sleeping in the recliner wearing flannel pajamas.

* * *

The giant 14 pound jackass who is wrecking my tree.

* * *

Dear fellow Wal-Mart shoppers,

This time of year means tempers are short so we need to establish a few ground rules. I'm already flushed and sweaty because 1) I'm menopausal. 2) I don't like crowds. 3) I don't like Wal-Mart. 4) Pushing this big cart full of crap is the most exercise I've had all week. 5) Wal-Mart has ignored my requests to screen people and have special shopping hours for normal people. So please observe the following rule: if you are close enough that I can touch you then you are in my personal space and by entering said space, you agree to forfeit all rights to bitch if things get ugly for you.

* * *

Now is the "fun" part of wrapping Xmas gifts- when you are trying to make sure the kids all have the same number and dollar amount of gifts. Then you keep finding things you forgot you bought, which screws up the aforementioned math you worked so hard on. So you have to go shopping again. And so on, and so forth up until after lunch on Christmas Eve when it is ok to start drinking if you are the mom.

* * *

"Where in the *hell* are my scissors

and who used all the F*&KING tape

Fa-la-la-la-la, la-la-la-lah."

* * *

42- The age at which you are too old to sit "criss-cross-applesauce" on the floor for three hours wrapping gifts.

* * *

Liz: "Can I borrow your snowman Christmas sweater? It's ugly sweater day at school tomorrow."

Me: "Yeah but it's still out in the barn with the Christmas decorations until we put up the tree this weekend."

Liz: "Oh. Well then can I borrow that red one you wear all the time with the scarf?"

Me: "Are you calling my regular sweater ugly?"

Liz: "No, it's not ugly. It's just....."

* * *

Me: "That's funny, Marshall, you must've read my mind. I was totally just thinking that I wish someone would wake me up at 4:45 A. freaking M. to watch *'Spongebob Christmas'* again."

* * *

Me: "Carter, you need to lose the attitude. You *are* aware that it is almost Christmas and the number of presents Santa leaves you is related to how good you are, right?"

Carter: "Yeah, but the gifts I really want are the ones I asked you and dad for so that doesn't matter."

* * *

Best silver lining about having an autistic kid: we have to take the tree and all the other crap down before we go to bed on Christmas night or else Marshall will wake up tomorrow morning, see the tree, and expect it to be time to open presents all over again. Which is good, because the cats were all fixing to get euthanized if the tree stayed up another night.

* * *

I am watching a lot of *'Toddlers and Tiaras'* during Christmas Break. I just watched a flamboyantly gay man put mascara on his six year old daughter. This is what I am reduced to. Christmas break is too damn long.

* * *

I just looked at the calendar and there is something really, really, really awry here. It says that even though Christmas is completely over, my kids are going to be at home for TWO more weeks for no apparent reason. This. Is. So. Wrong.

Chapter 21

Dysfunction is a relative term...

The women in my family are the funniest people alive. I have a crazy grandmother who thinks she is perfectly normal, and a mom who is also crazy but pretends she is perfectly normal. My sister and I are crazy but still recognize normal when we see it, and my three daughters and my niece are crazy and wouldn't know normal if it smacked them upside the head. When we are together, we all talk at once. I don't know if other packs of females do this, but I suspect they do. It is probably an evolutionary tool that people with uteruses (uteri?) have that enables them to mother multiple children at once. We can be telling a story about something that happened three years ago last November, and all of us speak at once, and we all hear each other at once. The men in my family are my dad, who has a hearing problem, my husband, who has a hearing problem, and my son Carter, who has a hearing problem. My other son Marshall, my brother-in-law, and my two nephews manage to avoid us when we are all together. I assume the hearing loss and the avoidance issues are also evolutionary, or maybe they are defense mechanisms that our men have developed over years of trying to ignore us.

My Niece, My Sister, My Daughter, Me, My Other Daughter, My Other Other Daughter, My Mom

---

I am no longer the most beautiful woman in my family. I used to be, but then my daughters grew up. I may be slightly biased, but I think those three young ladies are gorgeous. They are like new, improved models of me. Before I got all old, cynical, and bitchy.

I hate having to choose between 'fat and happy' and 'thin and homicidal'.

I want to be just like my great-grandma. She knew that life is short so she stayed ready to meet Jesus. She read her Bible, loved dirty jokes, and had the biggest *real* boobs I've ever seen. She dipped powdered snuff, but hid it in an old prescription bottle so no one would know (everyone knew). She carried a little revolver in her purse before the words 'concealed' and 'carry' were ever used in the same sentence, and she outlived nearly a half-dozen husbands. She always said "come here and hug my neck because I won't live much longer." She lived to be 95, so we were all legitimately shocked when she actually *did* die. Miss me some Grannie Rea.

I would like to thank all my female kin who have recently examined photos of my "falling down the basement stairs" injuries and provided excellent medical advice. Between us, we possess a vast array of medical knowledge gained from watching Grey's Anatomy, taking science in college, owning horses, being married to a Farrier, taking small children with disconcerting symptoms to various pediatricians, and numerous emergency room visits, since we are all accident prone. If anyone ever asked me "Do you have a doctor in the family?" I would feel totally comfortable saying "Yep!"

The text messages shown in the image:

> if you are old enough to have an iPhone you are old enough to put a glass over a bug.
>
> I'm working on it.
>
> I DID IT!!!
>
> And I can't believe it took me all morning to get the courage....
>
> thank. jeebus.

I read a romance novel one time and the heroine had the coolest name ever, so I named my first born child after her. Kiernan has been complaining about her name since she was old enough to have to spell it for other people or correct their pronunciation of it. Sucks to be her. I gave birth to you; I get to name you. It's a rule. Look it up.

Today I am reading an article Kiernan sent me from the Journal of Neuroscience entitled 'Autism and Abnormal Development of Brain Connectivity'. *This* is what having exceptionally smart daughters will get you. Why can't I just have an out-of-wedlock grandbaby to take care of like everyone else my age?

It has taken me twenty-five years, two husbands, and five kids to figure out that, for better or worse, the greatest gift my mother ever gave me is that she never compromised herself, nor sucked up to make me love her. I am so tired of seeing grown women make fools of themselves to impress teenagers.

––––––––––

How we stay connected in my family:

Friday, October 21, 2011 at 3:15pm CDT Emily Your Sister wrote on your timeline.

Are u alive? I haven't seen a single facebook post from u today!

––––––––––

There is a reason that pioneer people let their daughters get married at age twelve. It was so that they did not have to raise them when they were teenagers.

––––––––––

This. Is my new favorite quote: "Anyone who has ever had sex knows that porn is completely a show and nothing like real sex." It's from my oldest daughter.

––––––––––

I love it when you see the people you love often enough that you don't cry when you hug them goodbye.

––––––––––

A David's Bridal store commercial is on T.V. Liz says "Wow. I've never actually been to a wedding before! Well, except for yours, but I was in your stomach".

Dear bitchy teenage females: I not only wrote the book on being a bitchy teenage female- I still have the whole thing *memorized*. I can and WILL out-bitch you. Just think of me as the 'Bitch Queen Mum'... If you don't believe me- just ask *my* mom!

Me: (talking about plans for tomorrow)

Liz: "Arrrggghhhh! Oh my god. Oh. Wow. Aurgh!"

Me: "WHAT?!?"

Liz: "You just sounded *exactly* like Aunt Emily!"

Me: "I know. She's my sister..."

These are my sweet grandparents who died together in a car crash on September 11, 1989. I'm glad they never had to live a day without each other, and it's been long enough that they'd probably have already died from natural causes, but boy, do I wish they'd lived to see all of their great-grand kids. My maw-maw was the sweetest, kindest, most selfless woman I've ever known. The thing I remember most about her is that at every family dinner she would always sit on the floor because she just wanted everyone else to have a seat at the table.

My paw-paw was very quiet. He was missing half an ear, which I always found fascinating! He was a war hero and the kind of man you don't find much these days. The thing I remember the most about him was that he chewed tobacco and spit into a coffee can. If you have grandkids, it won't be the Christmas presents you buy for them, or the big fancy trips you take them on that will mean the most to them. It will be the littlest, most insignificant things that they will treasure as memories when you are gone.

Is it wrong that I'm debating making the hour-long drive to see my only sister this week because she is recuperating from knee surgery. And is on a pain drug pump. And it will be hysterical to talk to her when she's high. And I may or may not be planning to make a video. And put it on YouTube.

Please Note: My mother would like for me to clarify that while all of the other women for FIVE generations on the maternal side of my family are bat-shit crazy, it somehow managed to skip a generation and *she* is, in fact, normal.

Chapter 22

Just call me Jessie James...

Me: "Marshall, how was your second day of school?"

Marshall: "Well, I am not naked anymore."

Marshall: "Are you a bank robber?

Me: "No. I'm cleaning the bathtub and I have this red bandanna on my face so the bleach won't make me have an asthma attack."

Marshall: "Why are you robbing a bank?"

Me: "I am not robbing a bank. I am cleaning the bathroom."

Marshall: "Are you going to rob a bank?"

Me: "Yes. As soon as I am done cleaning the tub."

Marshall: "Why are you going to rob a bank?"

Me: "Because I need the money..."

———————

Autism silver lining #342: Taking the boys to see family for Thanksgiving in a small, small town. I can promise you that *no one* was ever so excited to be vacationing in Heavener, Oklahoma! My favorite aunt and uncle and cousins live there. They are chicken farmers and have one of those ATVs that looks like a hopped up golf cart. They raise puppies and have a few horses and all kinds of neat rocks and sticks and stuff. It's like Redneck Disneyland. Call my Uncle Jerry for reservations.

Marshall has a new stim. (A stim is a thing that an autistic person does to calm themselves. They will do a random thing compulsively for months or years, or until you've had enough and cut off whatever body part is involved.) This one involves clicking his throat and then exhaling loudly twice. He's been doing it 24 hours a day for the last 8 days. I don't know what it's called, but I need to find a name for it so the coroner will know what to put as my cause of death.

Dinner with 'Autism' and 'Autism Lite':

Me: "Marshall, say the prayer, please."

Marshall: "No."

Me: "Marshall- let's pray."

Marshall: "I don't know how." (Translated: I don't particularly want to)

Me: "God is Great..."

Marshall: (silence)

Me: "God is Good..."

Marshall: (silence)

Carter: "Marshall- did you forget your lines?"

Me (after I quit laughing): "Carter- can you finish it?"

Carter: "letus thankim for our food, by his hands we all are bred, give us Lord our daily dread."

I hope God remembers that it's the thought that counts.

———————

Carter won the MMA fight to see who was going to push the elevator button at the museum today.

———————

If you ever want to totally freak yourself *all* the way out, listen to an autistic person talk in their sleep.

———————

Proof that autism and puberty are a disturbing combination: When Marshall is hurt, he still wants to be held and comforted like a toddler. Today he fell in the driveway and skinned his knees. I sat him on the couch and asked him if I needed to kiss his knee. He said yes, so when I kissed it, his new manly black leg hairs touched my cheek.

———————

If you think it is hard walking away from a 4-year-old sobbing for you to not leave them at school, try it with a 13-year-old.

———————

Me: "Carter! Go with Elizabeth! She'll get your purple Kool-aid!"

Carter (Instantly freaking out because he is terrified of purple Kool-aid):
"Whatnoidontwantanypurplekooliadbecausepurplekoolaidisgross andi...."

Me: "I MEANT MARSHALL!!!"

Carter: "My name is not Marshall, it is Carter!"

Me: "I am aware of that. I just said the wrong name."

Carter: "Why do you forget our names?"

Me: "Because I am old."

Carter: "Then you need to take some medicine so you won't be old anymore."

Me: "Sign. Me. Up."

Today was "Serial Killers Get in Free" day at the zoo, apparently.

After school today while the kids were watching *Spongebob*- I laid on the couch and dozed off, which happens any time I am horizontal. I woke up abruptly because Marshall was sitting next to me gently tracing the lines in my forehead. Thank God it was with his finger and not a pencil. Or a pen. Or a marker. Or a sharpie.

_____

Neurological disorder or no, 13 is the official age at which having your son try to snuggle with you in bed is creepy. It's less "Aw, that's my sweet baby boy", and more "Oh my God! A masked intruder has broken into my house!"

_____

Things I've said today: "I don't have any idea where your Spider-Man mask is. It's seven o'clock- go back to sleep!", "You *cannot* eat chicken you found on the book shelf. Spit. It. Out!", "Do *not* throw that cat at me!", "I am *not* gluing the legs back on Woody right now. How did you find that in Dad's underwear drawer anyway?", and "Great, now my hair smells like chicken."

_____

Ask most people if they could go back in time and pick one day in their lives to 'do-over' and they will probably have to mull it over for a while... I can name mine instantly. I would go back to the day that I loaded up my perfectly normal, healthy 2-year-old son and took him to the doctor for shots. Autism is the suckiest thing that ever sucked.

_____

Marshall (watching Blue's Clues): "Who is barking at me?" (The correct answer is 'Blue'.)

Carter: "Scarlett. She's barking because she is sad because Hag died and he is buried in the back yard but his soul is in Heaven so it's ok but she's just barking because that is what dogs do because they can't talk like people do."

This Conversation Brought to You by 'Both Ends of the Autism Spectrum'.

———————

I think all 'Autism Awareness' bumper stickers are stupid. There is just no way you can fit the number of words it takes to explain autism and what needs to be done about it on a bumper sticker.

———————

To save my family the grief and expense of an autopsy, I try to keep everyone updated of my impending cause(s) of death. Today it is a heart attack, brought on by my dangerously high blood pressure because Marshall is OUT OF CLEAN BROWN SHORTS and I am trying to convince him to put on a non-brown pair. So far, I am not winning.

———————

Question: "What is it really like having two kids with autism?"

Answer: "Today, I get home with the kids and I have to pee after an hour in the car rider lines. I go into the bathroom and see that my 13-year-old autistic kid with the dubious potty-training skills has an upset stomach and has made an unspeakable mess in the bathroom and then left. I get him back into the bathroom and clean him from mid chest to knees, clean the toilet and the sink and wash my hands like I am scrubbing for surgery. I have used half a pack of adult baby wipes, so I take the trash outside and see that the trash I left on the porch before I went to get the kids is still on the front porch and if I put another one out there it will look tacky so I put on my shoes and take both trash bags around the house to the big trash thingy. Then I go back inside to pee and see that his shorts and underwear are still on the bathroom floor, so I take those to the laundry room and notice that the dryer has stopped. So I switch out the laundry, start a new load with his poopy pants, and fold the dry clothes on my bed. Then I take my daughter's part of the clean clothes to her room and see that her closet looks like a pyschopath hung up the clothes, so I enlist her help to straighten them out, which leads to us going through the whole closet to get rid of the things that are too small and too summery. Then I un-hanger those clothes and put half in the Goodwill box in the basement and the others in the 'summer clothes' container in the laundry room closet. Then I notice that the laundry has stopped again so I switch those out and silently pat myself on the back that I have just put the last load of dirty clothes in the dryer so I am going to get to skip doing laundry this weekend. Then I fold the second load of dry clothes and go downstairs to fix Marshall a drink. I notice that the kitchen I cleaned while they were at school smells like poop, so I make him go back to the bathroom, and see that he has once again pooped all over the toilet seat. I strip him down, clean him up again, send him to get clean shorts, underwear, and a shirt this time. I clean the toilet and the floor, and then scrub my hands raw. I take the dirty clothes to the laundry room and realize that the closet-cleaning created another half load of "dirty" clothes (which means they fell off her hangers and cats laid on them). So I go back upstairs and see that there are approximately 4 dozen hangers on my bed, and piles of hangers drive me totally insane, so I straighten them, count them into stacks of ten, and hang them up in the laundry room closet. I head back upstairs, and realize I am no longer wearing a bra. Since I am menopausal, I have a really bad habit of randomly breaking out into a flop sweat, ripping off my bra (and socks if I happen to be wearing them) and leave it in random places. I go into the bathroom, assuming that is where I have left the bra, and see that the cat has peed on the floor. I clean up the cat pee, take out the trash again, and then as I am washing my poor hands, I remember that I HAVE TO PEE! Which is what started this whole thing. I locked the door and peed. I washed my hands again and noticed that we are almost out of hand soap. As I headed downstairs to add soap to my grocery list, I saw the computer and realized that at least I have another good Facebook status.

———————

Adventures in autism: We haven't really had to have "The Talk" with our sons. Today Marshall asked me "What is a girl?" and I replied, very matter of factly, "Someone without a penis." The look on Carter's face was Ab. Solutely. Price. Less.

———————

That fancy ride-thru car wash in Tulsa is a fun family outing. Until it breaks down while you are right in the middle of it with your whole car covered in soap with one autistic kid who has to pee and one who gets scared and starts screaming like a banshee.

———————

Today is mine and Kenny's fifteenth anniversary. First marriages have a statistical divorce rate of 41%. For second marriages it's 61%. For parents with one autistic kid it is 81%. I can't even find a statistic for parents with two children with autism. We beat the odds again and again, even though we got married after only knowing each other a few months. It is a crazy life, but we must be doing *something* right.

———————

We went out to dinner tonight. With Marshall. And my parents. Past his bed time. I didn't *used* to be a 'Medicinal Marijuana for Autism' advocate. After finally sitting him on the floor under the table and telling him he was in the "box of shame" like the girl in *'Despicable Me'*- I would like to announce that I will be running for elected office on the 'Legalize Marijuana Pills for Autistic People' platform.

———————

Things I have said today: "MARSHALL! I DO NOT SPEAK SPANISH! SO I DON'T KNOW WHAT YOU ARE SAYING AND SAYING IT LOUDER IS NOT HELPING WITH THAT!!!"

———————

So Liz (my daughter, the aspiring actress) is telling me about the script for the non-Disney version of Peter Pan. She's explaining to me about how Peter and the lost boys never grew up. It's a long drawn-out story, but she stops herself right in the middle and says "Well basically- the whole thing could just be about an autistic boy, because Peter seems a lot like Marshall." Profound, my dear, profound.

———————

Marshall will not keep his clothes on and Carter has no modesty. I feel like I am living in a nudist colony, only without the volleyball games and fruity tropical drinks.

———————

Things I have actually said today (To Marshall): "I don't CARE if it's your Birthday. It is not ok to poop in your pants." (To Carter): "I don't care if Marshall is eating 'scary fruit snacks'. It is NOT ok to lay on your floor and eat Ceasar salad with your fingers." (To Liz): "I don't care if you were late getting in the car because you had to reach into the toilet because your basket of makeup fell over. I had to disassemble the whole seat yesterday and bleach it in the bathtub to get the urine out of the screws and bolts because your brothers can't aim and I still made it places on time."

My morning so far: Chased a buck-naked man down the hall, changed his urine soaked sheets and comforter, fixed the underwear he put on backwards, had a domestic dispute about why animal crackers are not acceptable as a sack lunch, had to forcibly hold a man down to get his socks on, spent five minutes hunting a lost black Nike (because "it is not *white* shoes day"), got bit brushing another man's snaggly teeth, stepped on discarded wet pajamas, hunted for the lost sock to the last clean pair that I handed to him ten minutes ago to put on, got my ass chewed because "my jacket that is in the car is cold because you didn't warm the car up before I got in it," ran back inside to retrieve a backpack and cereal that a man left inside- after I said "make sure you have your backpacks and breakfast," and got totally incorrect and uninvited driving directions from a man in the back seat. You would totally think I was a home health care provider for a couple of invalid grumpy old men, not the mom of autistic boys.

Since Marshall turned 13, I have been having somewhat of a nervous breakdown worrying about the fact that his adulthood is approaching at a super-sonic pace. Having a 4-year-old with "classic autism" is nothing compared to having your own fully-grown Rain Man living at home all his life. I have worried and

198

prayed about it to the point that I am annoying even myself. Last night I had a remarkable dream. We have (finally) after buying and selling seven homes, found the one that we all love. It is short on bedroom and bathroom space, but the yard, location, kitchen, and living room are perfect for our family. We have a big basement/garage that is unusable for parking cars because it was built in the 1960s before people drove mini-busses! In my dream, we transformed our basement into an apartment complete with a full bathroom, bedroom/living room, and a kitchenette. We let Liz live in it through high school and then when she left for college we moved him into it and he had his own "home" but was still literally just right under our feet. In my dream, the kids were all grown. Marsh was still gorgeous, still not very tall, but was gentle, well-mannered, and somewhat self-sufficient. I woke up with a complete and total sense of peace. This. Is when being a Christian comes in handy.

———————

I call this photo "Reasons it is a Good Thing We Aren't Going to Have to Pay for College for Marshall."

———————

Chapter 23

Is that a flashlight in your pocket or...

I'm at the movies with the boys today. We drive here, buy tickets, pee, get popcorn, watch the commercials, and as soon as the lights go down, Carter whips out a teeny flashlight. He's always worried about the dark and apparently took it upon himself to bring his own light. But I still don't know where he was hiding it because his shorts don't have pockets and I certainly did not see it in his hands.

At the lab with Liz after a blood draw:

Liz: "It's time for my bandage to come off. Which trash can do I throw it in? The regular one or the biohazard one?"

Me: "The biohazard one. The bandage has your blood on it..."

Liz: "Oh, no. Someone could steal it out of there and use it to clone me!"

Me: "Dude, you watch waaaayyyyy too much '*Dr. Who*'."

Liz: "It's almost time for Blake's Mom's mission trip!"

Me: "That's awesome!"

Liz: "Yep. She's going to Africa."

Me: "No, she's going to Nicaragua."

Liz: "Duh... Nicaragua is *in* Africa."

Me: "So no gifted class this year, huh."

>>·<<

You have to love it when your daughter is talking smack in a text to her friend about how she's gonna talk her mom into something that her mom has already said no to and details her entire plan. And then accidentally sends it to *you*.

>>·<<

Keeping it real- Tate style:

Kenny (To Liz): "Are you going to be a band geek?"

Me: "She would, but she can't play an instrument."

Liz: "I was planning to be a Show Choir Geek but I got kicked out of the class because I can't sing."

Me: "You also suck at sports."

Kenny: "Well, you'll eventually find your 'thing'. It won't be modelling though, because of your nose."

Liz: "What's wrong with my nose?"

Kenny: "Nothing, your head just hasn't grown into it yet."

Me: "Hey! You can make fun of her teeth but not her nose. She has my nose!"

Liz: "Yeah, my teeth are awful." (To me): "Did you remember to call the dentist?"

>>·<<

Me: "Go stand by the Geese and I'll take your picture."

Carter: "I can't. They will peck my whole entire head off."

>>·<<

Sometimes I think middle-school math teachers assign homework so they can all get together and laugh at how bad the parents are at helping with middle school math.

>>·<<

Me: "Did your dad text you back?"

Liz: "No, did he text you back?"

Me: "Nope. Maybe he's been kidnapped!"

Liz: "If someone kidnapped him, they would've already brought him back."

Me: "Why is that?"

Liz: "Because he would've complained that their room was too dirty."

>>·<<

Elizabeth was speculating this morning as to whether or not her male "gifted class" teacher is married. So I said "Does he have any kids?" She said "No, but he has a nephew so he's probably married."

>>·<<

Me: "Carter, are you ready to swim?"

Carter: "Where is Dad?"

Me: "He's at work. Why?"

Carter: "Because he needs to swim with us, not you."

Me: "Why?"

Carter: "Because you are a boring swimmer."

Me: "I swim with you every day!"

Carter: "But you're just a *girl* so you can't throw us like dad does and that is the most fun."

Me: "Get. Your. Swim. Suit. On. Right. Now."

>>·<<

Going out to eat with your kids is way more fun when they are 20, 18, 15, 14 and 12 than when they are 10, 8, 5, 4 and 2.

>>·<<

I just made blueberry muffins. In case you didn't see the picture of them my daughter posted to Twitter.
#whydopeoplecarewhatsheiseating

>>·<<

I told Carter he was old enough to fix his own drink. Here is the glass he chose.

>>·<<

In the frontier days, girls got married at fifteen and started being mothers and homemakers. My fifteen-year-old daughter cannot figure out how to use a can of whipped cream without letting all of the air out, rendering it useless.

>>·<<

Does anyone have an upcoming colonoscopy, root canal, or water-boarding that they would be willing to trade places with me and take my kids to see *'Smurfs 2'*?

>>·<<

Conversation about what I should do on my birthday while the kids are at school:

Me: "I probably should stay home and clean the house."

Liz: "You should go eat somewhere and take me."

Me: "I am not taking you out of school- this is *my* day! Try again..."

Liz: "What about a pedicure?"

Me: "I don't like people touching my feet."

Liz: "What about getting your nails done?"

Me: "I touch too much gross stuff because of your brothers to have long nails."

Me: "I know! I will take the car to Tulsa and get it all detailed so it will look like new!"

Liz: "Mom. That is the saddest thing I have ever heard."

>>·<<

Easter morning negotiations: "You have to eat your Lucky Charms before you can touch that chocolate bunny." "Only the ears before church."

>>·<<

I can absolutely guarantee that no matter what happens today, I will be found not guilty by reason of insanity.

>>·<<

Packing up and taking my family in one car on an overnight trip is so much fun! -Said no parent of autistic kids and teenage girls ever.

>>·<<

Just let me apologize in advance to anyone who comes into contact with any of my children today. They have all lost their damn minds.

>>·<<

Carter: "Oooohhhhhhh. I just threw my back out."

Me: "You did? How..."

Carter: "Picking up a train."

Me: "Isn't 11 a little young to have a bad back?"

Carter: "It was a heavy train."

Me: "Oh, good. Another hypochondriac in the family."

>>·<<

Me: *"Carter, is this yours?"*

Carter: *"Yep."*

Me: *"What's it for?"*

Carter: *"Miss Kelli gave it to me."*

Me: *"But what's it for?"*

Carter: *"It's the instructions for how to make love."*

>>·<<

"Don't jump off the pool ladder!" "Don't jump off the pool ladder!" "Don't jump off the pool ladder!" "Don't jump off the pool ladder!" I think the only thing keeping me sober this summer is knowing that at some point I am going to have to drive someone to the emergency room.

>>·<<

Dragging information out of my son is not unlike being a CIA interrogator:

Me: "Did you have a good second to last day at school?"

Carter: "Yes."

Me: "What did you do today?"

Carter: "We practiced our act for the talent show."

Me: "There's a talent show? Do you have a *note* for me by any chance?"

Carter: "Yes."

Me: "What is your act?"

Carter: "My class is doing the 'Cup Song'."

Me: "Awesome! When *is* the talent show?"

Carter: "Tomorrow at 12:30 p.m."

Me: "Well, would you like for me to *come*?"

Carter: "No thanks, I'm good."

Me: (Slaps myself in the forehead as I realize this is how I missed Field Day last week...)

>>·<<

Babysitting my computerized "grandbaby" (Home Ec project), whose "mother" (Liz) has declared it to be "overly dramatic". This, my friends, is the very definition of the word irony.

>>·<<

So. You know how we blamed all our crazy after we had a new baby on hormones? Well, we weren't correct. It's lack of sleep that screwed us up. My daughter was up all night with the Home Ec baby and she's a total weepy mess today. I *almost* feel guilty for hoping that she got one with colic.

>>·<<

More irony: When a child you stayed on bed-rest for months and months to gestate, lived in the hallway of the NICU for days and days praying for, and managed to raise successfully and safely for 15 years- looks at you disapprovingly as she takes the computer baby away from you because you are NOT HOLDING IT RIGHT! I hate friggin' Home Ec baby.

>>·<<

I changed my mind. I am not really all that disappointed that I am not going to have very many grandkids. Having a new baby of your own is fine. Trying to help one of your children with a new baby when they decide that the whole thing is just a way for them to point out everything you did wrong with them and make you feel inadequate is not really very much fun. Did I mention that Home Ec baby went back to her cabinet at school today? That was the most annoying weekend in the history of weekends.

Chapter 24

What you CAN do...

As I am writing this, it is "World Autism Awareness Day". It's a day of platitudes and promises, lots of empty words and *some* genuine concern. The government is playing politics and throwing my tax dollars at brain research. People with kids who are "on the spectrum" are wearing their kids' disability like a badge of honor. Autism is the flavor of the week. When all of the politicians, entertainers, and media types have moved on to the next "sexy" disorder, I'll still be here- still unable to look at photos of Marshall before age 2, before his shots, when he was perfectly normal- before the autism. And I'll still be here- still trying to convince people that my other "high functioning autistic" son isn't really even the same thing as autistic- he's just a little different. Still wondering what caused this and still dealing with it when it wakes me up each and every morning before my alarm goes off.

People often ask me what I would like people to do for/with kids like mine. There's not actually all that much that anyone can do. I don't think autism is as huge an epidemic as all the hype indicates. *Way* too many "weird" kids are being diagnosed as "on the upper end of the autism spectrum". But...what you *can* you do? Here are my thoughts:

1) Ask someone with autistic kids what they think about vaccines. Listen to them with an open mind. I can show you pictures and videos taken days before Marshall's 2 year shots and ones taken within days of the mega-vaccine visit. It is a totally different child. Period. I believe there is a genetic predisposition to autism and the vaccines somehow trigger it. Carter has never had any shots. He is also diagnosed on the autism spectrum but is significantly more "normal" than his older brother. I used to hate taking the kids to the doctor until I finally found a nurse practitioner who doesn't feel the need to browbeat me like I am an imbecile for not vaccinating them. Never try to talk another mom or dad into *or* out of vaccinating their kids.

2) Don't email, text, paste, or call the parents of an autistic kid when you see something on the news about a new cure or treatment for autism. We spent the first six years after Marshall's diagnoses and thousands of dollars trying to figure out how to fix him. When I found myself researching Chelation Therapy, where they replace the kid's blood, I realized that I had lost my mind and there was ABSOLUTELY NOTHING that was going to 'fix' my kids. I have been much happier since I stopped paying attention to the cure of the week. I am very *(very)* well educated about each and every legitimate and quackery thing out there. He is rarely sick, and I firmly believe that God has Marshall in hand and protects him from the minor illnesses that normal kids deal with. I will never attend a support group, so don't ask me please! I had to make a decision to remember that I have more 'normal' kids than autistic kids, and a husband, so autism *cannot* define me. I am NOT the "Mom of an Autistic Kid"; I am the mom of five kids.

3) Don't tell me all about your cousin's neighbor's sister's kid with autism. I am busy enough trying to handle my own, and "If you've seen one autistic kid; you've seen one autistic kid". It's not that I don't care about other autistic people, but I don't have time to worry about them. On the other hand, if you know a parent with

211

an autistic kid who is struggling and needs someone talk to who has been there, then I'm your girl!

 4) I post things about them all the time on Facebook. It is not because I want sympathy or attention. It is because they are freaking hysterical! The best thing you can do for us is what you already do, click "like" or comment to let us know that you enjoy hearing about the absolute craziness that happens each and every day. Knowing that I have Facebook friends who care about my family makes it easier somehow.

5) Do for the special needs families in your life what my sister does for me. She has sons the exact same ages as Carter and Marshall and she never makes comparisons about our kids and never makes me feel like my boys are somehow "less than" their peers. She applauds their small accomplishments just like I applaud my nephews' more typical ones! She also makes me glad that we don't have to do any sports, because going to all those games and practices sounds like a living hell to me.

6) If you know a family with both autistic and 'neuro-typical' kids, be sure to include *all* the kids in your conversations, prayers, and activities. My daughters have to deal with a lot as siblings of autistic brothers. It has made them very compassionate and patient young ladies. They are also very independent, because of all the times that their needs have had to hit the back burner because of the boys. I admire them all so much.

 7) If you know the parents of any special needs kids, be sure to compliment them on their amazing ability to stay married and to stay out of jail for killing each other. Kenny and I have been blessed beyond measure to have each other through this. The biggest *(THE BIGGEST)* "miracle treatment" we have been able to

give Marshall is a constant, predictable, firm family unit. Because I'd been married before, we had high risk pregnancies back to back to back, sick preemie babies, lost Kenny's parents way too soon, and then the autism, we have defied the statistics by just sticking together. If you know a family like ours, offer to babysit if you think you can handle it. We need time together more than most people, and we also need time away from each other more than most people!

8) Don't ever take it personally if you have never set foot into our home or if you invite us somewhere and we say no. Especially when he was younger, Marshall couldn't handle having other people in our house and going to other people's houses was a supreme challenge. It was also very heartbreaking for me to be around groups of people with "normal" kids his age. If you run into us at the store, church, or school don't take it personally if we "blow you off" by keeping our carts and kids moving. Stopping with them in public can be the kiss of death. Just trust me on this.

9) If you are close friends with the mom of an autistic kid, invite her to go to lunch, dinner, shopping, wherever with you. You will have to invite her 158 times that she can't or won't go for each one time that she *does*. It will be worth it to her though, just being asked.

10) If you are a teacher or school employee, do what the ones we've been so blessed with do. Don't ask me *what* they do because it is too much to name! They are phenomenal. If you know a Special Ed Teacher- buy her a spa day. Seriously. You couldn't pay me enough.

And in conclusion:

People ask me what the hardest thing about having autistic kids is. They are often surprised to hear that it is not the day to day grunt work involved in keeping them safe and happy. The hardest part, and the thing that keeps me up at night, is thinking about the days to come when I am not there to protect them. I see men in prisons and homeless shelters and such and I *know* that many of them are just grown up versions of my sons who have been thrust into a world they are not equipped to handle alone. *Please* keep that possibility in mind in your own communities. Think of how innocent and naïve a preschool-age child is and now picture that level of brain function in the man you see wandering the streets talking to himself. I don't know what causes autism, and I sure as hell don't know how to fix it. I used to question why God would allow my children to have this affliction, then I remembered when I was in the middle of the world's nastiest divorce and I was lying face down on the floor in a lake of tears and begging Him to let me find one person, just one, on this whole damn earth who would love me unconditionally...

He gave me two.

Oh, and as it turns out- the problem with Carter's nipples was that he was wearing a shirt with a big vinyl decal inside-out on a super cold day so it was rubbing him raw.

The end.

215

Made in the USA
Lexington, KY
21 February 2014